HIS NAME FOREVER

The Story Behind the Name of "God"

By: Iris A. Foreman

authorHOUSE®

AuthorHouse™
1663 Liberty Drive
Bloomington, IN 47403
www.authorhouse.com
Phone: 1-800-839-8640

First published by AuthorHouse   06/16/2011

ISBN: 978-1-4490-4029-1 (sc)
ISBN: 978-1-4490-4030-7 (e)

Library of Congress Control Number: 2011900456

Printed in the United States of America

Any people depicted in stock imagery provided by Thinkstock are models,
and such images are being used for illustrative purposes only.
Certain stock imagery © Thinkstock.

This book is printed on acid-free paper.

Scripture taken from the NEW AMERICAN STANDARD BIBLE®, Copyright © 1960, 1962,
1963, 1968, 1971, 1972, 1973, 1975, 1977, 1995 by the Lockman Foundation. Used by permission.

Contents

Acknowledgements

A book like this is not the work of one person alone but a culmination of influences, teachings, and conversations with many persons. I have been blessed to have people at various stages in my life who have imparted valuable nuggets that have encouraged me and, even, to some degree, shaped my thinking. I appreciate every teacher, friend, spiritual advisor or leader, and pastor who shared, in sincerity, their understanding of spiritual matter.

The impetus for the research that resulted in this book began with my husband, Anthony P. Foreman. His courage and wisdom to question the status quo challenged me to look beyond the doctrine of the church. Without his support and encouragement, I may never have gone on the spiritual journeys that have led me to the path of truth I now walk.

Many thanks to my brother, Darryl X McKenzie, author of *Black, White & Easy,* who encouraged and mentored me in publishing this book. I even have him to thank for the awesome book cover design. Not only is he an accomplished author and poet but also an artistic genius. I would like to recognize my sister, Renee McKenzie Hayward, PhD. From childhood on to adulthood, she alone was the one who read through my short stories and poems, much as she does today — with great patience and tolerance.

I must acknowledge Luis Ascersion, a former co-worker and friend, who has significantly impacted my awareness and understanding of the name of our Creator. Though Luis was not the first to reveal the name to me, he was the first person I knew to consistently call the Almighty by His name. For many months, I enjoyed beautiful fellowship with Luis and his congregation as we acknowledged the Almighty and His son by their sacred names.

This book benefited from the editorial work of Pamela Guerrieri. She and the team at Proofed to Perfection took the time to understand my nonconventional subject matter and edited without challenging my voice or message. Pamela assured me that *His Name Forever* would be "a polished, professional book that will open readers' eyes to a whole new level of understanding." I like to believe that this is and will be the case.

My parents, Grover and Sara McKenzie, deserve special thanks for so many things that they have done for me throughout my lifetime. However, here I would like to thank them for teaching me at an early age to think for myself. It was that sound advice that helped me to break from blindly accepting traditional teachings and delve into a search for truth. I thank the Most High for blessing me to have been born to such wonderful people.

Preface

I DECIDED TO WRITE ABOUT THE NAME OF the one whom two-thirds of the world calls *God* following my graduation from seminary. Surprisingly enough, the inspiration for this topic did not come from my Master in Divinity program studies but from my life experiences shortly afterward. There is nothing like simply living to open our eyes to truth.

There are a few key things I want to point out before you read through these pages. You will notice that I do not always hold to convention or political correctness. The terms that I use in this book reflect my current beliefs about the Almighty and the Scriptures. For example, I believe that the Creator of the heavens and earth, written about in the Holy Bible or the Scriptures, is above all in the universe. One of my ways of honoring Him in my writings is by capitalizing the first letter of every pronoun I use in reference to Him. Also, I have no qualms and make no apologies about using the masculine pronoun for the Almighty. Although I believe that the Almighty is spirit and has no sexual designation, I am comfortable with masculine references to Him and choose not to flip-flop between masculine and feminine pronouns.

My studies have led me to accept that the Israelites—the descendents of Abraham, Isaac, and Jacob—were Hebrews. They were referred to as *Hebrews* and *Israelites* in the Scriptures. In some places, the word *Judeans* (stemming from the Greek word Ἰουδαῖοι, which is very loosely translated from the Hebrew word *Yehudim*) is used to describe Israelites from the area of Judea. Following the Babylonian captivity, the area of Judea consisted of the territory west of the Jordan River. Later, it was the southernmost province of Palestine during the Roman occupation. Although Bible translations may sometimes have the word *Jews* in it, that word is not a true translation from the Greek or Hebrew words used to refer to the Israelites. So, I purposely do not use the word *Jew* when referencing Hebrews or Israelites. However, I do use the word *Jew* when referring to people who practice a form of religion called Judaism.

I use several terms to refer to the Almighty, whom most of our Bibles simply call *God* or *the Lord*. I am not comfortable with either of these two terms, as the contents of this book will explain. So, I use such words as the Most High, the Mighty One, the Power, the Creator, the Almighty, and even Heavenly Father.

You may wonder why I do not call the Messiah by his name. (This topic may warrant writing a whole other book.) Rather than use the name that people have ascribed to him based on Greek and Latin translations, I try to keep it simple by just saying Messiah. Of course, when I speak of the Messiah, I am referring to one of the main persons written about in the New Testament, the Son of the Most High.

In this book, I quote a lot of Bible verses. While in seminary, I used the New American Standard Bible (NASB). I like this translation because it is a fairly sound translation from the Hebrew and Greek texts. Having studied both languages, I feel confident with how closely the NASB Bible verses reflect the original languages. For this reason, unless otherwise noted, all quotes from the Bible will be from the NASB.

I use *the Scriptures* and *the Hebrew Scriptures* interchangeably when referring to the portion of the Bible commonly known as the Old Testament. These were the holy books of the Israelites and what the Messiah and apostles read, studied, and preached.

It is important to me that once we come to know certain truths that we begin to walk in them. It is my goal to honor the truth that I have come to know and to help others in their quest for greater truth.

Introduction

Bless the LORD, O my soul; And all that is within me,
bless His holy name! (Psalm 103:1)

"*B*LESS HIS HOLY NAME..." THERE IS JUST something about these
words that seem to pull at the heart strings of those who love
the Most High. A beautiful hymn was composed using these very
same words. Although simple, these words carry a heavy message.
Those who take ownership of these words declare their allegiance,
commitment, and deep love for Him. His name alone is recognized
and declared as a true reflection of His greatness. All of His attributes,
I have been told, are embodied in His name. Therefore, the name of
the Most High just ought to be blessed.

I remember singing these words and wondering what they really
meant. What is "His holy name" that my soul should be blessing?
Somehow, I instinctively knew that *God* was not His name nor was *the
Lord*. Yet, I had been accustomed to hearing Him called *God* and *the
Lord* as well as other names during my many years of Bible study. So
the pool of names I could choose from was pretty extensive. But which
of these names were truly His holy name? I knew there had to be one

name that was uniquely His that the psalmist had in mind when he wrote this particular psalm. It had to be a name that represented the fullest essence of the Most High. So, just what is that name?

Even after I came to know the answer to that question, nothing changed for me. I continued to refer to Him as *God* and *the Lord,* as the importance of using His holy name escaped me. I used His name intermittently, but with no commitment. After a while, I returned to my old habit of not acknowledging His name in my studies, conversations with others, worship, prayer, and meditation—just as if I had no knowledge of the truth.

Like me, some people have been told His true name, but the relevance of His name was not emphasized; therefore, they had no conviction to use it in the place of the terms *God* and *the Lord.* There are, of course, other people who just have never been taught His name at all and, therefore, have a legitimate excuse for not using it. They cannot be expected to use what they do not know, can they? However, the vast majority of people, I believe, fall somewhere in between these two positions. Most have heard so many different names for Him and are just plain confused as to the relevance of one name over another. So, quite naturally, they continue to call Him *God* and *the Lord.*

We are in a time in the course of history when much that was hidden before is now being revealed. Over the years, society has experienced social and technological advances, moving from the Agricultural Age to the Industrial Age, to the Information Age, and finally to where we are today — the Communication Age. With each transition, more people gained access to literature and art as well as the time to enjoy them. In past eras, arts and information were available only to a select few, usually the wealthy, intellectuals, and clergy. However, in this modern era, information is available to almost everyone, especially those who have access to the Internet.

In regards to just theological information, more people now have access to Bibles and Bible-related books than ever before. From the time of the printing press, Bibles have been available for laypeople, but not all could read, purchase, or had the luxury of time to read them. Today, Bible reading is not left to the clergy only; laypeople have personal copies of the Bible and actually read them from time to time. Many laypeople are searching the Scriptures themselves for a better understanding of life and the giver of life as they seek to improve their lives.

So, it would seem that there is little logical reason why so many of us are still ignorant about something as basic as the name of the one we claim to worship. All of this data that is now available has made us more informed about the happenings in our world than ever before. However, when it comes to understanding the Bible and knowing the name of the Most High, for the most part, we are no better off than those people living in the Agricultural or Industrial ages. Dare I even say, when it comes to this subject, we hardly even have a leg up on the people who lived in the Dark Ages.

Why is this? We have our Bibles, Bible dictionaries, encyclopedias, and many other Bible study tools. Despite having all of this information, many of us overlook the key pieces of information that reveal not only the Most High's name but also the importance of His name. In reality, it does not take all of these different study aids to unearth His true name. We can ascertain His name and its significance just by opening and reading the very Bibles we carry around or have sitting on our shelves or coffee tables.

For almost 2000 years, there has been little change in the way people learn and comprehend biblical concepts. We continue to rely on others to tell us what is important in regards to faith matters. Those who we turn to for spiritual direction are often church leaders, pastors, theologians, and Christian teachers. Naturally, they mainly pass on what they themselves have been taught to be important. Unfortunately, the Most High's name was not one of the important facts passed along. For most Christians, the primary emphasis on what is spiritually important is to know Jesus. And when it comes to names, most people are told that the only name that matters is the name of Jesus. Actually, most people could read the Bible from Genesis to Revelation, the entire content of the Old Testament and the New Testament, without a clue as to the name of the Most High. In what is called The Lord's Prayer, it is this name that even the Messiah, himself, reverenced when he said "Our Father which art in heaven, hallowed it be thy name…" (Matthew 6:9 KJV).

The bottom line to all of this is that, throughout the years, it has become acceptable to have a higher power that was identified merely as *God* or *the Lord*. It is acceptable to the church leaders and to the people who choose to worship Him. But what about to the Most High? Do you really think it acceptable to Him for us to just call Him *God* or *the Lord*? The clergy and church leadership over the past twenty centuries have developed Christian and church doctrine as well as dictated the direction of Christian thought. They have largely done nothing to enlighten the public on the Creator's name and its importance. Laypeople, meanwhile, have not made a hearty effort to demand to truly know the holy name. But His name is important. After all, the Almighty proclaimed His name from the mountaintops when He revealed Himself to Moses.

Appointed by the Most High to lead the Israelites, His chosen people, out of their enslavement in Egypt, Moses had developed a unique relationship with Him. This close relationship was necessary, for there was much that the Most High needed to teach His chosen people so that they would know how to properly worship Him and live in the land He had promised to them. Moses was the man chosen to speak the Mighty One's words to His people. As this fascinating relationship developed, Moses longed to see the Mighty One's face and boldly asked this of Him. Although he did not get to see Him face to face, Moses saw Him pass by as He declared His own name in a moving self-proclamation (Exodus 33:18–34:8).

The Mighty One of Israel has never kept His name from us. If He made His name known then, why don't we know it today? Who has kept it from us and why? Those were the questions I struggled to find answers to as I began this journey of finding the story behind the name of *God*.

This book is written as an introduction to some readers and a reintroduction to others to the Heavenly Father by His name and not just His character. As you read the upcoming chapters, you will be able to see how that "great" and "wonderful" name became buried over the years and tucked away from many Bible readers and believers. You will be challenged to consider three questions. First, why was the name kept from people? Second, who benefited from this? And, last, what possible harm has been the result of this concealment? As you come to see and note the name in the Scriptures and understand its importance, hopefully you will come to the conclusion that your own understanding, worship, and walk would be so much different if you knew and appreciated the "great" and "wonderful" name of the Mighty One of Israel.

This book will settle the mystery of His true name. It is He of whom the Bible is written and of whom the world has come to know as the *God* of Abraham, Isaac, and Jacob. In revealing His name, this book will try to encourage respectful, reverent usage of the name by those who claim to have or seek a relationship with Him.

It is a contradiction of word and action when we say that we have a relationship with someone and yet choose to engage in personal dialogue with that person or being without addressing them by name. Also, an evaluation of true worship will need to be considered when such worship is devoid of calling out by specific name the one to whom we are giving adulation.

Consider these verses from the Scriptures and draw your own conclusions about the importance of the Most High's name.

His name is Great...

> Also concerning the foreigner who is not of Your people Israel, when he comes from a far country for Your name's sake (for they will hear of Your great name and Your mighty hand, and of Your outstretched arm); when he comes and prays toward this house, hear in heaven Your dwelling place, and do according to all for which the foreigner calls to You, in order that all the peoples of the earth may know Your name, to fear You, as *do* Your people Israel, and that they may know that this house which I have built is called by Your name. (1 Kings 8:41–43)

> "I will vindicate the holiness of My great name which has been profaned among the nations, which you have profaned in their midst. Then the nations will know that I am the LORD," declares the Lord GOD, "when I prove Myself holy among you in their sight." (Ezekiel 36:23)

His name is Holy...

> You shall not profane My holy name, but I will be sanctified among the sons of Israel; I am the LORD who sanctifies you. (Leviticus 22:32)

> "For the Mighty One has done great things for me; and holy is His name." (Luke 1:49)

So, what is that great and holy name? Let's find out.

Chapter One:
The Trap of Worshiping
the Unknown *God*

Wᴴᴱɴ ᴛʜᴇ Aᴘᴏsᴛʟᴇ Pᴀᴜʟ ғɪʀsᴛ ᴇɴᴛᴇʀᴇᴅ ᴛʜᴇ ancient city of Athens on his second missionary trip around 50-51 A.D., he could not help but notice the many temples and monuments honoring the various Greek deities such as Zeus, Athena, Apollo, and Hermes. "So many monuments for so many gods," he probably thought upon his arrival. Born and raised in the Hebrew culture, in which there was only one who was worshiped (Deuteronomy 6:4), Paul of Tarsus most likely began to consider the differences between the Greeks and his own Israelite people. He may have also taken time to examine the similarities. After all, people in both cultures believed that something greater than they controlled the world. The paramount difference was that the Greeks believed in plural powers while Paul's people believed in one power, the Most High.

As Paul traveled about the Grecian city, according to the biblical account, he came across a monument set up for an "unknown god." The Greeks—being a polytheistic, superstitious people—believed that different gods or powers influenced different areas of their lives.

For example, one power ruled the sun while another had an ability to grant wisdom. So, just to cover all the bases, the Greeks made provisions for a power that they might have overlooked by constructing a monument to the "unknown god." In a public forum, Paul called the people's attention to this so-called "unknown god" whom they had acknowledged in their ignorance. He declared that this power, who was "unknown" to the Greeks, to be none other than the Creator of the heavens and earth and all who dwell therein (Acts 17:16–31). This power was the Mighty One of the Israelites who had been the deliverer and salvation of their patriarchs, Abraham, Isaac, and Jacob. This was the Mighty One that many Gentiles in the first century had come to worship alongside the Israelites in the synagogues—not just in Jerusalem but also in many other cities throughout the Roman world. He is the same Holy One that the Messiah and his followers worshiped. The Greeks did not know the identity of this power by name until Paul revealed Him to them.

Many people who read and believe the Bible today are no different from these ancient Greeks. They have read and heard about the Mighty One whom they refer to as *God*, but in many respects He remains unknown to them. They worship a power whom they know not by name but only by general titles or common terminology. The word *lord* is a mere title, and the word *god* is a common term. Contrary to what many people believe, such titles and terms do not truly identify a specific power that people choose to worship. Christians across the world find themselves unable to tell the personal name of the Most High. And, when pressed to come up with a name, they may mention Jesus or Jehovah. Some may even say He has many names and may refer to Him as El Shaddai, the Ancient of Days, the Almighty, or some other name or term used to describe Him in the Scriptures. None of these are His true name, however. Take notice that in most places of worship today, the Almighty's name is not even mentioned. I would dare say that the name of the Mighty One is probably the most secretive non-secret that exists. This is sad, especially considering that His stated desire has been for people of all nations to know and worship Him (Psalm 86:9, Isaiah 2:2–4).

Common Terms Used for the Most High

When we open the first book of the Bible, Genesis, we are introduced to the Creator of all things, the Most High, whom our English Bibles identify simply as *God*. The very first verse in our Bibles identifies Him as such. Actually, the English word *god*, used to refer to Him in the Scriptures, is translated from the Hebrew word elohim (pronounced e-loh-heem). *Elohim* is a plural form of the word *el*.[1] *Elohim*, however, is what He is and not His name. *El* means "power" or "might."

Elohim is a general term used for the Most High as well as for other "mighty" or "powerful" beings such as idols, angels, or even human rulers who are perceived as great[2]. For example, the word *el* is the name of the high power among the Canaanites. This simple word is actually common to the Hebrew, Aramaic, and Arabic languages, yet the origin and root from which the word was derived is obscure. Both *el* and its plural, *elohim*, were used before the earth was destroyed by the flood when only Noah and his family were the sole human survivors. These words, *el* and *elohim*, continued to be used after the great flood, as well.

In Genesis 31, for example, the word *elohim* is used in reference to idols. This chapter relates the story of an encounter between Jacob and his father-in-law, Laban. Jacob was the grandson of Abraham, the Hebrew whom the Most High called to leave his family and go to a land that He would show him. Among those whom Abraham left behind was his brother Nahor. Through the years, Abraham fathered Isaac, and Isaac became the father of Jacob. Meanwhile, Nahor fathered Bethuel, and Bethuel became the father of Laban. When Jacob came of age, his parents wanted him to have a wife from their own family. Jacob ended up settling down with the two daughters of his kinsman Laban, Leah and Rachel.

Although the family of Abraham and the family of his brother Nahor shared the same bloodline, spiritually they were different. Abraham had a direct encounter and covenant with the Most High, and he and his descendents worshiped and served this one power. However, Nahor's family, of whom Laban was a descendent, continued in pagan worship like the people among whom they lived.

After living with and working for his father-in-law Laban for many years, Jacob packs up his family and his livestock and leaves without word to return to the land of his birth. Without Jacob's knowledge, Rachel, Jacob's beloved wife, takes some of the idols from her father's house and packs them with her belongings. When Laban realizes that Jacob has departed, he soon discovers that some of his idols are missing as well. Upset over his discovery, Laban runs in pursuit and approaches Jacob to inquire why Jacob left in secret. Laban then asks Jacob, "Now you have indeed gone away because you longed greatly for your father's house; but why did you steal my gods?" (Genesis 31:30). The word translated as *gods* comes from the same Hebrew root word *elohim*. In this passage, the term *elohim* refers to the idols. Clearly, Laban is not referring to the Most High but instead to portable household objects of worship.

Another example of the term *elohim* used in reference to so-called powers or idols occurs in the book of Exodus when Moses leads the Israelites out of Egypt. The Israelites are the descendents of Jacob, whose name was changed to Israel. Moses gathers the children of Israel together to tell them the commandments of the Most High. He tells them to listen, learn, and observe so they can obey the statutes and ordinances that the Most High commanded as part of His covenant with them. Moses begins to repeat the very words given him. He quotes, "I am the LORD your God who brought you out of the land of Egypt, out of the house of slavery. You shall have no other gods before Me" (Deuteronomy 5:6–7). Here again, the word translated as *gods* is from the Hebrew word *elohim*. It is interesting to note that the words "your God," referring to the Most High, come from the same Hebrew word *elohim*. In this particular instance, the word has a different Hebrew ending that is specifically used when including the second person possessive pronoun *your*. In Hebrew, a pronoun suffix is added to a noun to indicate the possessive. This is unlike English, in which the possessive pronoun is a word separate and distinct from its noun.

So as you can see, the English translations of *el* and *elohim*, as used in the Old Testament, can be used to refer to any mighty power in general. Similarly, the English word *god* most commonly used to translate these terms can refer to a pagan deity or even idols. Many Christians learn as children that the word *god* refers to the Most High when the first letter is capitalized, i.e., *God*. This method does help a reader to identify Him when reading the Scriptures. However, a listener must learn to differentiate the general from the specific by carefully discerning the context of what is being said.

Therefore, the specific entity that this term refers to depends on the intention of the speaker or writer. For example, a Christian, Muslim, Hindu, and tribal religionist all may use the word *god* to refer to their respective mighty ones, but the identity of each power is not necessarily clear to the listener or reader because the term *god* is so general. However, if they each called their mighty one by his personal name, then the identity of that power would be certain.

The English word *god* and the Hebrew word *elohim* are common nouns, not proper nouns. For example, a man may have a son whom he names Johnny. He may address him as "son." However, "son" is not his name. "Son" essentially describes who Johnny is to that man. In fact, almost half of the world's population may claim ownership to the term "son" because all males are sons of someone. Even though Johnny may be called "son" by others who hear his father calling him that, "son" is not his personal or proper name—regardless of whether you capitalize the S in the same way that people capitalize the G in *God*.

Another term used in the English translations of the Scriptures to refer to the power who created the heavens and earth is *Most High God*. This term is translated from the Hebrew words *El Elyon*. We have already indicated that *el* has been translated in our English Bibles as *god*. The second Hebrew word in this descriptive term is *Elyon*, which, among its many other meanings means "high" or "most high." This very descriptive title that is ascribed to the Creator of the heavens and earth by the writers of the Scriptures suggests that the Mighty One of Israel was not the only recognizable power that people acknowledged. To say that He was the high or most high power implies the notion that other lesser powers either existed or were thought to exist. Any Old Testament reader would be able to name at least one or two powers that the pagan nations and, at times, Israel worshiped. Among the forbidden powers were the Baals, Asherah, Molech, Chemosh, Egyptian gods, and others.[3] The books in the New Testament also reveal that people believed in the existence of other mighty ones besides the Mighty One of Israel just as we saw in Acts when Paul went to Athens and saw all the monuments to the Greek deities. So for us to say *we worship or love*

God, as many of us are or have been quick to exclaim, really imposes on the listener to ask, "Which one?"

Are You Worshiping the Unknown Today?

The Most High, the Creator of the heavens and earth and the deliverer of Israel, clearly distinguishes Himself from these other *elohim*. The whole discourse of the Scriptures is evidence that this has been His objective as He sought to be worshiped by all of his creation. By revealing Himself to Abraham and his descendents, He intended that people would come to know Him as the only one to be worshiped. Remember what He said to Moses on Mount Horeb and Moses recounted to all the Israelites.

> I am the LORD your God who brought you out of the land of Egypt, out of the house of slavery. You shall have no other gods before Me. You shall not make for yourself an idol, or any likeness of what is in heaven above or on the earth beneath or in the water under the earth. You shall not worship them or serve them; for I, the LORD your God, am a jealous God... (Deuteronomy 5:6–9)

The Mighty One of Israel was not in denial that people worshiped other *elohim*. Given the writings throughout the Old Testament, there is no reason to assume that the Israelites did not believe in the existence of other powers besides the Most High. It is very apparent from reading the history of the Israelites that they suffered from temptation to worship the different idols of their neighbors. However, the teachings of Moses centered on the worship of the Almighty alone.

When issuing the commandments to the Israelites, the Most High was emphatic about being recognized as above the others. In that same address to the people, Moses said, "For the LORD your God is the God of gods and the Lord of lords, the great, the mighty..."

(Deuteronomy 10:17). The Mighty One of the Israelites is the chief *el*. There may be others (and there are), but He is over them all. That was then. And, if it is true that there is nothing new under the sun, then it is still true today. He is *El Elyon*, the Most High power.

Today, there are still many different *elohim* that are worshiped, although their names are different from the false *elohim* we read about in the Bible. Muslims believe in a supreme power whose name is Allah. The Hindus believe in a supreme power who they call by the name Brahman. The Sikhs refer to their power by the name Waheguru. The supreme power of the ancient religion of Zoroastrianism, which is still practiced today, is called Ahura Mazda. People all over the world worship something that they believe to be a greater power. Many of them call their objects of worship by specific names as well as refer to them simply as *god* and *lord*, just as Christians and Jews. The difference, however, between many people who worship the Most High of the Bible and people of other religions is that the latter seem to know their mighty ones by name. They call on that name in worship and invoke it in prayer. Whereas, the average Christian has no clue about the name of the one he or she worships.

The *elohim* of Abraham, Isaac, and Jacob still seeks to be set apart and worshiped as the one true and living *elohim*. But how effective is that worship if we do not call Him by His name?

Chapter Two:
The So-Called Names
of the Most High

THERE IS A WIDESPREAD SCHOOL OF THOUGHT that the Most High actually has more than one name. Almost any book you pick up on this subject—written by Christian theologians, scholars, pastors, etc.—will list a variety of names that they say are His. Although all of the lists will have some names in common, too often each list is unique to its writer. As a perfect example, consider this very book. Here, I refer to the Most High Elohim also by such terms as the Creator, the Mighty One, the Almighty, the Power, and so on.

When it came to identifying the one whom the Israelites worshiped, the writers of the Bible saw Him in different ways depending on the situations they were experiencing. Sometimes, Elohim was their deliverer, covenant maker, warrior, provider, healer, holy one, fortress, etc. Throughout the history of mankind, and specifically the history of Israel, Elohim met the needs of His people. Each writer had his own individual, personal views and experiences with Him. Therefore, the writers of the Scriptures used many different descriptive terms to describe Him.

If you took every one of these terms and formed a list, that list would be quite extensive. So, when people today prepare lists of names of the Most High, they tend to select the most frequently used terms found in the Scriptures. They are also influenced, to some degree, by their own individual preferences based on personal experiences with Him. In addition, some people have even formed names by taking an attribute and converting it into a name. Such so-called names were never clearly stated in the Scriptures as the name of Elohim. If we see a list that has 21 of these names (or 8 or 200 or some other number), we can be sure that the list simply comprises His characteristics and is not all-inclusive of the many ways He was addressed or described in writings. Yet despite this, there is only one true name for Him. It is the only one name that matters.

Plethora of "Names"

The following lists have some of the titles and names we are likely to see in writings about the Most High of the Scriptures. However, many of these titles and names are not restricted to the Most High. There are some common titles and names that many people use to refer to their deity or deities. Some of these titles and names are descriptions used to speak of the Most High's character and awesome qualities. Other titles and names were made up or fabricated.

Some names have been based on mistranslations, misinterpretation, or misunderstandings but appear as proper nouns. A substitute name, on the other hand, is a name to be used in the place of His real name. Then, there are compound names or terms. Some of the most common ones are those that consist of one of the substitute or formed names and a descriptive term.

Still, none of these names are the one name that He declared as His.

Titles or Common Names

Abba – Hebrew, meaning father. *"Abba! Father!"* (Mark 14:36)

Adonai – Hebrew, meaning master or lord. *"I saw Adonai sitting on a throne."* (Isaiah 6:1; 'Lord' is translated from Adonai)

El – Hebrew, meaning might or power. This is often translated as "god." *"Eli, Eli..."* (Matthew 27:46; Eli translates to *my El)*

Elohim – Hebrew, meaning might or power (plural of *el*). This is often translated *God* when referring to the *el* of the Israelites and is translated *gods* when referencing two or more powers.

Father – Found frequently in the New Testament. *"Our Father who is in heaven..."* (Matthew 6:9)

God – Found throughout the English Old Testament and New Testament.

Heavenly Father – Found in the New Testament in some translations such as New American Standard Version. *"... your heavenly Father is perfect."* (Matthew 5:48)

Kurios – Greek, meaning lord or master. Found in the Septuagint (Greek translation of Hebrew Scriptures; Septuagint discussed in greater detail in Chapter 5.), word is used in the place of Adonai. In the English New Testament, almost 100 percent of the time "Lord" is written, it was translated from the Greek word *Kurios*.

Lord – Found in English translations throughout the Old Testament and New Testament. Also printed with all capital letters, as "LORD."

Substitute Names

These words are some of the names that have been used in the place of the proper name of the Most High.

Ha Shem – Hebrew, meaning The Name. This substitution was used in the place of the actual name. It was never meant to be the name of Elohim but only a substitute to be used.

Jehovah – Non-Hebrew name assigned in post-biblical times. This word was created as an assumed translation of the name found in the actual Hebrew Scriptures.

Jesus – Non-Hebrew name assigned in post-biblical times. Traditionally, this name is ascribed to the Messiah in the English Bibles. Some Christian doctrines seem to teach that this is the Mighty One of Israel's New Testament name. The belief is that this name supersedes any Old Testament names for Him because the Messiah declared that, *"I and the Father are one,"* (John 10:30). Also, John 5:18 and 8:56–59 are used sometimes to support this.

Descriptive Terms

These terms are derived from words used in the Scriptures to characterize the many qualities of the Mighty One. They were never presented in the Scriptures as His name but merely as descriptors. In using these words, the writers draw attention to the Most High's unique, noteworthy attributes.

Almighty – Found in the Old Testament: *"I am God Almighty"* or *"I am Almighty God"* (Genesis 17:1)

Ancient of Days – Term used in Daniel 7

Compassionate and Gracious God – Translation of terms that the Most High used to describe Himself and that others used concerning His character; appears in some translations as "Merciful and Gracious" (Nehemiah 9:17, 31, Psalm 86:15)

Consuming Fire – Found predominantly in the Old Testament: *"For the LORD your God is a consuming fire..."* (Deuteronomy 4:24)

Creator – Found in the Old Testament and New Testament to identify the one who created the heavens and earth: *"...your Holy One, The Creator of Israel..."* (Isaiah 43:15)

Deliverer – As in *"...You are my Help and my deliverer..."* (Psalm 40:17, 70:5)

El Shaddai – Hebrew, meaning El Almighty or El All Sufficient; found in Exodus 6:3, although most versions include English translation of God Almighty: *"I appeared to Abraham, Isaac, and Jacob as El Shaddai..."*

Everlasting God – As in *"...he called on the name of the LORD, the Everlasting God"* (Genesis 21:33)

Faithful God – Term used to further describe the Father in Deuteronomy 7:9: *"...the faithful God, who keeps His covenant..."*

God of Truth – *"...You have ransomed me, O LORD, God of truth"* (Psalm 31:5)

Holy One – Found frequently in the books of Psalm and Isaiah: *"...I am the LORD your God, the Holy One of Israel..."* (Isaiah 43:3)

I AM – The phrase that the Almighty used in Exodus 3:14 in response to Moses: *"...say to the sons of Israel, 'I AM' has sent me to you"*

I AM that I AM – Sometimes seen as "I AM WHO I AM" depending on the translation; the Almighty used this phrase in response to Moses: *"God said to Moses, 'I AM WHO I AM...'"* (Exodus 3:14)

King – Many references to the Most High as King, even the King of Glory: *"Who is the King of glory? The LORD strong and mighty..."* (Psalm 24:8)

Lawgiver – As the one who prescribed laws, statutes, and commandments to Israel, this was an appropriate term used to refer to Him: *"The LORD is our lawgiver."* (Isaiah 33:22)

Majesty – Word found in both the Old Testament, often to describe something pertaining to the Almighty or His creation, and in the New Testament as a direct reference to Him: *"… at the right hand of the Majesty on high"* (Hebrews 1:3)

Most High – Term used frequently in the Old Testament and occasionally in the New Testament; sometimes this term is used in conjunction with *God,* as in the *Most High God*

Potter – Term used occasionally to describe Him from the analogy of the potter and the clay found in Jeremiah 18

Redeemer – Term found in the Old Testament; a very familiar quote from Job 19:25 refers to the Most High as such: *"I know that my Redeemer lives."*

Righteous One – Term to describe Him: *"…Glory to the Righteous One…"* (Isaiah 24:16)

Savior – Describing the Mighty One of Israel in the Old Testament: *"…my stronghold and my refuge; My savior…"* (2 Samuel 22:3)

Substitute Names with Descriptive Terms

Each of the descriptive terms used in combination with the substitute name, Jehovah, is a translation of a Hebrew word that was in the original Hebrew Scriptures. Some English translations of the Bible include some of these combined terms.

Jehovah Elohim – Combined terms mean Jehovah Mighty One ("God"); translated often as Lord God

Jehovah Jireh – Combined terms mean Jehovah Who Provides: *"Abraham called the name of that place Jehovahjireh…"* (Genesis 22:14, KJV)

Jehovah Nissi – Combined terms mean Jehovah My Banner: *"Moses built an altar, and called the name of it Jehovahnissi"* (Exodus 17:15, KJV)

Jehovah Raphe – Combined terms mean Jehovah Who Heals: *"...for I am the LORD that healeth thee"* (Exodus 15:26, KJV)

Jehovah Sabaoth – Combined terms mean Jehovah of Hosts; found many times in the Old Testament, such as *"...for the LORD of hosts was with him"* (1 Chronicles 11:9, KJV)

Jehovah Shalom – Combined terms mean Jehovah Our Peace; the place where Gideon built an altar: *"...he called it Jehovahshalom..."* (Judges 6:24, KJV)

Jehovah Tsidkenu – Combined terms mean Jehovah Our Righteousness: *"...he shall be called, THE LORD OUR RIGHTEOUSNESS"* (Jeremiah 23:6 KJV)

Despite having used different words and terms for the Most High, the Scripture writers (Moses, David, Solomon, Isaiah, Ezra, Jeremiah, etc.) also used His personal name. It is this personal name that we should strive to become familiar with and to use when addressing Him. This is the name that He chooses to be called and known by.

Chapter Three:
The Language of the Scriptures

I N ORDER TO FULLY APPRECIATE THIS WHOLE discussion on the name of the Most High Elohim, it is important to know a little about Hebrew, the language in which most of the Old Testament text was originally written. Then, we can begin to understand how we ended up with our English translation. More specifically, we will look at the word *god* that is used to refer to the Most High in our English Bibles. Was the word *god* even used in Hebrew? Where does the word originate? What does it mean? Does this word *god* accurately reflect who or what is the Almighty? These all are questions to consider as we try to get to the heart of knowing the correct nomenclature for Him.

The Bible was written by many different people over a period of several hundred years. The first section, commonly referred to as the Old Testament, is also known as the Tanakh or the Hebrew Scriptures. It is, essentially, a compilation of writings that tells the history of the Creator and His people—including how He created man, His unique relationship with mankind, and how that relationship was destroyed by man's disobedience to the Creator—and then goes on to foretell what is to come in the course of time. In these same Scriptures, we see the re-establishment of the relationship between the Creator and mankind. The Most High initiates this relationship building through Abraham and his progeny, the Israelites, giving them instructions for living, worshiping, and restoring their on-again/off-again relationship with Him.

As previously mentioned, the term we often see in the Scriptures as *God* is a translation of the Hebrew word *El.* This is an ancient word that is found in the Hebrew vocabulary. We know that the Israelites used the words *el* and *elohim,* and it is believed that Abraham did as well. Even Abraham's first son—whom he had with his wife Sarah's maid, Hagar—was given the name Ishmael by the Almighty. Note that this name contains the word *el.* Ishmael means "El hears." Therefore, we see that the term *el* is an acceptable term used by the Most High in reference to Himself in the days of Abraham (Genesis 16:11). Later, Abraham's grandson, Jacob, was given a new name by a messenger of the Almighty that also contained the word *el* (Genesis 32:28). Jacob's new name was Israel, which means "El strives" or "he who strives with El."

The writing of the first five books of the Scriptures—Genesis through Deuteronomy—are chiefly credited to Moses, a descendent of Abraham the Hebrew and an Israelite. He was raised in the house of the Egyptian king or Pharaoh and was adopted by the daughter of the Pharaoh after she discovered him as an infant floating in a basket down the Nile. This was during the period in Egypt when the Pharaoh had ordered all Israelite male babies to be killed. The Egyptians had begun to fear the Israelites because this people who had come to Egypt with only seventy in their number now outnumbered the Egyptians. The fear that they would be overtaken led the Egyptians to enslave the Israelites (Exodus 1:9–14). When Moses became an adult, Elohim selected him for the great work of not only delivering the Israelites out of their bondage but also to speak the Most High's words of instruction for how the people were to live an acceptable life. Later, Moses wrote an account of history as he was told by Elohim and as he experienced. He wrote in Hebrew because he was writing to Hebrew people.

Moses used the term *El* to describe the Most High. Although Moses spoke to the Israelites and even wrote in the Hebrew language, the word *el* is not an exclusive Hebrew word. It is a word that was used from a period that, in all likelihood, preceded the existence of the people who have come to be known as the Hebrews. The word *el* is found in the names of some of Cain's and Seth's descendents in Genesis 4 and 5. For example, Mehujael (4:18) means smitten of el (god).

This can be easily understood when you consider that before there were many languages, there was but one language. The biblical account written of Noah tells us that the only persons who survived this worldwide flood were Noah, his wife, Noah's three sons, and the sons' wives. It is a fair assumption that this group of eight was able to verbally communicate with each other by speaking the same language. In all likelihood, the language that Noah spoke after the flood was the same language that he spoke before the flood, and possibly it was the same language his forefathers spoke (namely, Lamech, Methuselah, Enoch, and, maybe, as far back as Seth and his father, Adam).[4] It is conceivable that Adam and his wife spoke in a language that they later taught their children. It was this language of man, the first man, that Noah possibly spoke, being himself a direct descendent of Adam. When we consider the longevity of Adam's life and the many subsequent generations born during his lifetime, it raises the probability that his language continued throughout his own life span and, even, among his own direct descendents.

Adam lived until he was 930 years old, and everyone in his line, prior to Noah, lived a considerable amount of years while he was still alive. According to calculations based on the Scriptures, Noah's father, Lamech, was born during Adam's 874th year. He was 56 years old when Adam died. Given Lamech's age, he was old enough to have learned and communicated in Adam's language. Think about this: Most people speak their parent's native language unless they are raised in a different culture where another language is spoken and their parents do not pass on their native tongue. It is possible that whatever language Adam used was also used by his progeny, from Seth all the way to Noah. See the following chart derived from the genealogy recorded in Genesis 5. For each of Adam's descendents, it shows Adam's age when the descendent was born.

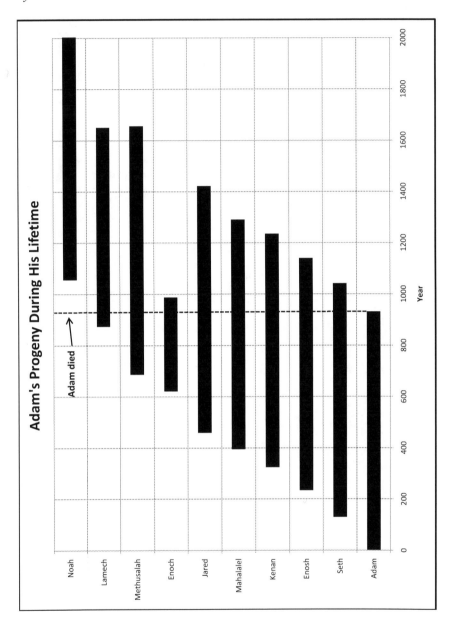

When the floodwaters receded and Noah and his family left the ark, Elohim told them to multiply and replenish the earth. According to the Scriptures, that is exactly what they did. So, as time progressed, the earth's population increased and everyone spoke the same language as Noah (Genesis 11:1). That is, until the day that the whole earth's population joined together to build a city and a tower that would reach heaven. This act displeased the Most High, and it was at this point that He confused the people's speech so that they were no longer able to understand each other (Genesis 11:6–9). Consequently, the people scattered and spread out across the earth, speaking different languages.

If Noah and his sons used the terms *el* and its plural *elohim* in reference to the Almighty, then so did their descendents after them who, when all speaking that one language, decided to build the city and the tower. Therefore, it is possible that when the language of man was confounded and multiple languages ensued following the incident of the Tower of Babel (Genesis 11:1–9), some people may have retained this particular reference to the Most High. This is probable considering that the word *el* was used by various peoples in the ancient world and also by the fact that, in most cases, this term meant power, might, strength, or some similar type of reference. Given that *el* appears in more than one language with similar meanings, it may point to the possibility that it, indeed, stems from the original language that existed before the Tower of Babel. Of course, this cannot be proved emphatically, but it does present itself as a possibility to be considered. So, perhaps Noah and his sons did use *el* when referring to the Most High, and perhaps, after the people of Babel scattered, some people continued to speak the original language of Noah while others spoke variations of that language.

El in the Hebrew Language

Putting aside this speculation, we do know that *el* and *elohim* were present in ancient Hebrew as well as in many other ancient languages including Aramaic, Arabic, Akkadian, Ugaritic, and Phoenician in some cognate form. These languages fall under a group of languages that have been identified as Semitic. The Semitic language is a subgroup of the ancient Proto-Semitic languages. Semitic refers to the descendents of Noah's eldest son, Shem, who are known as Semites. Therefore, the Semitic languages are thought to be the languages of those who were descendents of Shem. Today, the Semitic language is a subgroup of what was once referred to as the Hamito-Semitic language group but now has been renamed as the Afro-Asiatic language group. The vast majority of these languages are spoken in parts of Africa, in the Middle East, and in parts of Asia.

In the ancient world, the Hebrew speakers shared words in common with other Semitic languages. It is the Semitic language, of all the language groups, that is believed to have the longest history of all languages. The following illustration diagrams the many languages of the ancient world that made up this Proto-Semitic family of languages.

Notice where Hebrew is on this language tree. When you consider that the people speaking these languages lived in close proximity to each other, it is conceivable that there was some overlapping of words. It is also within the realm of possibility that there were some words found in many of these subgroups that originated from the top of the language tree. The word *el* may be one of those core words.

There is no way for us to know, definitively, which was the original language of Noah of all the languages that were spoken after the Babel incident. Also, there is no way of knowing if the people, after having the languages confounded, were able to remember the particular term they once used to speak of the Most High. We do know that the term *el* has ancient roots. The actual ancient word may not be positively determined because, over the years, languages change. "The original patterns of specific words very often shifted to other patterns during the separate histories of the various languages after they branched off from their ancestral subgroups... Because of these pattern shifts, it is usually not possible to reconstruct individual words back to Proto-Semitic, only individual roots."[6] It is the Proto-Semitic root of the words that can be reconstructed, and the original word, itself, may not be known with certainty. So, even though it may be possible to come to the conclusion that certain words come from the same stem, it is not always possible to know with all certainty what the original Proto-Semitic word was.

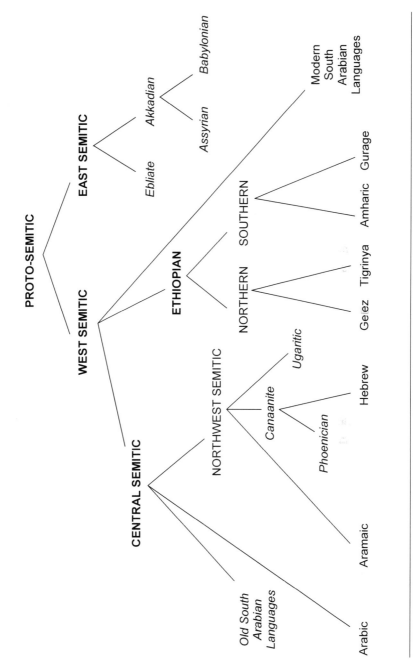

By: Iris A. Foreman

Road from El to God

Today, our English translations of the Bible generally do not have the words *el* or *elohim* but instead have the word *god* in its place. Actually, to say that *god* is a translation of the words *el* or *elohim* is wrong. The definition for *el*, as I said, is power or might. It was used to refer to judges, rulers, divine ones, angels, and idols—mighty ones or those with power. So, what does *god* mean? How did we get from *el* to *god*?

The Hebrew Scriptures were translated from the Hebrew language into the Greek language about five hundred years before the Common Era (B.C.E.) by a committee of seventy people. This Greek translation was known as the Septuagint. The Hebrew words *el* (and *elohim* when used to refer to the Almighty) was replaced with the Greek word θεὸς in the Septuagint. Converting these Greek letters into the English alphabet, this word is pronounced or transliterated as *theos*. The word *theos* was not a true, equal substitution for *el* and *elohim* because *theos* had its own meaning and connotations that were quite different from the way *el* and *elohim* were used in reference to the Creator. Certainly, both words, *theos* and *el*, were used to refer to rulers and powers that people perceived as "higher powers"—that is, higher than any normal human. Yet, *theos* referenced certain things in the Greek culture that the term *el* was never meant to in the Hebrew culture, especially when referring to the Almighty. Each culture had its own way of understanding life and the things of the world. So, the concept of a great power that rules over creation and whom the people worship would be different from one culture to another.

In the Lexical Aids to the New Testament under *Theos* 2316, it says as follows: "God. Originally used by the heathen and adopted in the NT as the name of the true God."[7] The Greeks used this term before it was ever applied to the Hebrew Scriptures in the Septuagint. The Greeks, we have established, not only worshiped many gods but also believed in the existence of all gods. They used *theos* to refer to the many gods in whom they believed. Therefore, when the translators of the Hebrew text were putting together the Septuagint, they used a Greek term for *Elohim* that was used in the Greek culture to represent the beings that possess powers and might over man's or the world's existence. For the Greek, that term was *theos*. Unfortunately, that term was associated heavily with pagan deities.

"The word *theos* seems to be from the Greek verb theô, which means 'to place'... The heathen thought the gods were disposers (thetêres, placers) and formers of all things. In using the pl. [plural] form, the Greeks intimated their belief that elements such as the heavens had their own disposer or placer... The heavens were the grand objects of divine worship throughout the heathen world as is apparent from the names attributed to the gods by the ancient Greeks."[8] Purportedly, every Greek *theos* or *god* had its own domain, its own part of life or the world that the Greeks believed that particular *theos* controlled and ruled. *Theos* does not adequately compare with the Hebrews' reference to the Almighty as Elohim, who was Creator and master of all and the giver of all life.

There are other inconsistencies that occurred when *el* or *elohim* was translated into *theos* in reference to the Almighty. Often in the original Scripture text, the Most High is referred to as Elohim, which is the plural of the word *el*. This plural is not to imply that He is more than one being, in any sense, but the plural is used to pronounce His majesty and greatness. "The use of the plural form with singular meaning is not unique to Israel. Similar forms occur in pre-Israelite Babylonian and Canaanite texts in which a worshiper wishes to exalt a particular god above others. This form has been called the 'plural of majesty' or the 'intensive plural' because it implies that all the fullness of deity is concentrated in one god. Elohim's being the most common word for God in the OT [Old Testament] thus conveys this idea."[9]

However, when the text was translated into Greek, the plural form was not transferred over to the Greek, for *theos* is singular.

> The Sept. [Septuagint] constantly translated the Hebr. pl. [Hebrew plural] name Elohim, when used for the true God, by the sing. [singular] Theos, God, never by the pl. [plural] theoi, gods. The reason for this was that at the time the Sept. [Septuagint] translation was made, Greek idolatry was the prevailing superstition, especially in Egypt under the Ptolemies. Their gods were regarded as demons, that is, intelligent beings

totally separate and distinct from each other. If the translator rendered the name of the true God by the pl. [plural] *theoi*, they would have given the heathen under the Greek culture an idea of God which is inconsistent with the unity of the divine essence and conformable to their own polytheistic notions.[10]

So, assigning the pagan title *theos* to Elohim in the translation of the Hebrew to the Greek changes the concept of Elohim to something other than who He had presented Himself to be to the Israelites. And it also presented Elohim in a different way than what the Israelites understood Him to be for them. Using the term *theos* for Elohim was for the convenience of the Greeks, who did not quite understand Him due to their particular worldview. Also, to the Greeks, the concept of a mighty power like the Mighty One of Israel was just foreign to them. The Israelite people were an anomaly to the Greeks, and it was thought that if they were able to read the holy books of the Israelites then they may be able to understand them better. Actually, this is the reason that the Scriptures were translated into the Greek language in the first place.

Following the Messiah's death and resurrection, during the period of the early Church, the Greek dominance in the world subsided. The Greek language was no longer the primary language in the "civilized" world. Many people who now worshiped the Most High spoke other languages and wanted to have the Scriptures in those languages. The Septuagint, which had gained popularity, was used by the followers of the Messiah, and, for many years, it was still used by non-Messianic Israelites. However, through the course of time, the Israelites who did not believe in the Messiah returned to the original Hebrew Scriptures, written in Hebrew, to separate themselves further from their brothers and sisters who were professing that the Messiah had come.

The followers of the Messiah did much to spread his message of the Most High Elohim to people in different parts of the world. It was no longer limited to the nation of Israel, but it was a message of hope that extended to all people of every nation. People gravitated to this good news and to the Most High, and as they did, there was a demand for the Scriptures to be written in languages that the new believers could read and understand. So, as the Scriptures were translated into various languages, the word used for the Hebrew word *Elohim* continued to change. Just as the transition of the word from Hebrew to Greek carried a pagan connotation, the same thing occurred, unfortunately, when the word was translated to Latin, Gothic, Armenian, Coptic, and other languages.

Because the first translators of the Scriptures, the Septuagint's committee of 70, sought to translate the Hebrew word *elohim* into a Greek term that reflected the Greek's unique culture and understanding of a mighty power, the stage was already set to do the same again when the Scriptures was translated into other languages. For example, in the Latin Vulgate—a 386 C.E. (Common Era) translation of the Hebrew Old Testament and the Greek New Testament into Latin—the word *elohim* is replaced with *deus*. The Latin *deus*, once again, is not a true translation of *elohim*. *Deus* is the Latin word that stems from the word *deiwos*, of the Proto-Indo-European language family. This word, which is said to mean "divine," shares the same root as the name of the chief European-Indo pantheon, which is essentially a temple of all the so-called deities. Also, it shares the same root as the name of the "god of the day-lit sky." So, the Latin term used to reference Elohim, the Almighty, falls woefully short because the Latin replacement *deus* brings the baggage of pagan religions.

This should provide some indication that translations of the Scriptures were not as pure as one would expect or hope for such sacred texts and, more specifically, in reference to the Most High. Unfortunately, translating words from one language to another has inherent and, often, unavoidable limitations. Sometimes comparable words just are not available. This poses a problem for the translator who seeks to convey the original meaning of a text when there are not appropriate, equivalent words to do so. Another problem is the issue of using terms that accurately portray meanings and concepts relevant to one culture to people of a different culture. To solve this problem, the new translation must be contextualized into words and ideas the new audience of people can identify with that fit within the context of their own, unique culture. For example, the Latin language translator may have debated on whether or not to keep the Hebrew word *Elohim* as the term for the Most High when there was not a comparable Latin term to convey the exact meaning of that Hebrew word. However, it may have been decided to use *deus* instead as a starting point to the reader who already understood the concept of a higher power. By using *deus* in the place of *el* or *elohim*, the Latin reader would be more likely to comprehend, in time, the special meaning for this particular being, even though he may have previously associated *deus* with a pagan entity. Nonetheless, whatever the reasons that resulted in the use of pagan names and titles in reference to the Most High, this practice continued from the first major translation of the Scriptures into the Greek and then to other language translations centuries later.

The Latin Vulgate was used in the Western world from the fourth through the fifteenth centuries. It was the only text that was sanctioned by the Roman Catholic Church. In 1380 C.E., however, John Wycliffe began the very first English translation of the Bible. However, because the printing press was not yet invented and the strong arm of the Roman Catholic Church opposed any Bible version besides the Vulgate, Wycliffe's English translation was not widely used. It is believed that he translated from the Latin translation. Instead of the Hebrew *elohim* or the Latin *deus*, Wycliffe used the word *god* in his Bible. This word *god*, we will discuss later, stems, possibly, from a totally separate word family and not the Proto-Semitic and the Proto-Indo-European language groups. It was a term we see in most of the English translations that followed Wycliffe's translation, and, of course, is what we see even today.

The following table gives a brief historical overview of Bible translations and the word used in each translation as a substitute for the Hebrew word *elohim*. Most of the Bible translations were done based on the Hebrew Old Testament text and the Greek New Testament text. In some cases, the Greek Septuagint also was used for what is considered the Old Testament.

When the Hebrew Bible was translated to English, the word *god* was used as a less-than-comparable translation of the word *elohim*. The English term *god* follows the pattern of substituting the Hebrew word and concept of Elohim with *theos* in Greek and *deus* in Latin. These substitute terms were used despite the idolatrous origins. This practice continues to occur in many of the translations of the Scriptures now available.

So what is this word *god* and where does it come from? Several sources show that there are various possible beginnings.

Estimated Time of Translation	Bible Version/ Translator	Word used for "Elohim"	Manuscript on which New Translation was Based
3rd to 1st century B.C.E.	Greek Septuagint/ Committee of 70	*Theos*	Hebrew
382 C.E.	Latin Vulgate/ Jerome	*Deus*	Hebrew OT & Greek NT
1382 C.E.	English Translation of New Testament/ John Wycliffe	God	Latin Vulgate
1522 C.E.	German NT/ Martin Luther	Gott	Hebrew OT & Greek NT[11]
1525-1530 C.E.	English Translation/ William Tyndale	God	Hebrew OT & Greek NT[12]
1535-1537 C.E.	Coverdale Bible/ John Rogers	God	German and Latin, possibly Tyndale's Pentateuch and NT[13]

The American Heritage Dictionary indicates that the etymological source of the word *god* is from the word g̲h̲e̲u̲(ə), which has Indo-European roots. This essentially means that this word comes from a grouping of many ancestral languages that fall under the heading of Indo-European. This particular word, *gheu(ə)*, means "to invoke" or "to call." Its noun form is *ghu-to*, which can be translated as "the invoked." Also from this word *gheu(ə)*, we get the word *giddy* from the Old English word *gydig, gidig,* meaning "possessed" or "insane." We also get the Germanic word *gud-iga,* meaning "possessed by a god." (See the note on giddy.)[14]

A more comprehensive source for the etymology of the word *god* points out that the precursor to the word comes from very pagan, unsavory origins. The following chart illustrates the various languages from which this word or word family was used. It looks back at each word that is believed to have preceded the word *god*. This chart gives some insight into the word, the language origin, and meaning. For example, the actual word *god* was written and spoken between 450 C.E.–1100 C.E. in what is considered "Old English," and the meaning assigned to the word then was "supreme being" or "deity." The exact origin of the word is not definitive, although the source is suspected to be either Proto-Germanic or Proto-Indo-European. The Old English word clearly comes out of either of these two language families.

The word *god* has its origin in pagan religions and was used in some form as a word to reference pagan deities who were invoked or to whom sacrifices were made. Even though *el* and *elohim* were also used in referencing entities other than the Most High, it was a term that was acceptable to the Israelites and to Him. The translation of this term to *theos* in Greek and *deus* in Latin and, then, from those terms to *god* in English may carry more baggage than we need when referring to the Almighty. For this reason, the word *god* is not used herein in reference to the Almighty except when citing quotations. The Hebrew words *el* or *elohim* will be used instead.

Table on Etymology of the Word God [15]

Language	Word	Meaning	Note
Old English, the English language as written and spoken c.450–c.1100.	god	supreme being, deity	
Proto-Germanic, hypothetical prehistoric ancestor of all Germanic languages, including English.	guthan		In this family of languages, we find variants in Dutch word god, German word Gott, Old Norse word *guð*, Gothic word *guþ*
Proto-Indo-European, the hypothetical reconstructed ancestral language of the Indo-European family. The time scale is much debated, but the most recent date proposed for it is about 5,500 years ago.	ghut- (root is gheu(e), a verb meaning to call, invoke)	that which is invoked	In the 4th century B.C.E. Sanskrit (Indian literary language) writing, we find a variation of this *huta-* "invoked," in an epithet of Indra, a Hindu god (the god of weather and war)
Proto-Indo-European	ghu-to- (root is *gheu, a verb meaning to pour a libation)	poured	

Chapter Four:
The Name

WHILE SHEPHERDING HIS FATHER-IN LAW'S FLOCK NEAR Mount Horeb, Moses saw a single bush burning on the mountainside. Curious about this strange-looking phenomenon, Moses approached the bush for a better view. It was then that a voice from the midst of the burning bush spoke to him. That voice turned out to be none other than the voice of the Most High. Elohim tells Moses that He has a special assignment for him. Moses was to be used by Him to deliver the children of Israel out of their bondage to the Egyptians and lead them to the land of Canaan that Elohim had previously promised their forefathers—Abraham, Isaac, and Jacob—well over 400 years ago.

Now, remember that Moses was an Israelite by birth but was raised in the Egyptian royal household as an Egyptian. Therefore, he was rightfully skeptical that he was the man for this particular job. Furthermore, Moses had left Egypt as a fugitive after he realized that others were aware that he had killed an Egyptian man. This murder was in defense of an Israelite who was being cruelly beaten by the Egyptian. Instead of the Israelites embracing Moses as their defender or supporter, he discovered that his noble actions were misunderstood.

He was not seen as the Israelite he was but as the Egyptian he was raised to be. So, fearing punishment for the murder he had committed, he fled Egypt to the land of the Midianites. It was here that he met and married the daughter of a Midianite priest.

To go back to Egypt to the very people whom he thought did not accept him was going to be a challenge in itself. But for him to say that he was sent by the Most High to deliver them and that the Mighty One that they worship was answering their prayers through him would require some hard proof. He may have wanted to be able to convince this people that his mission to lead them was legitimate and that he could be trusted. Therefore, Moses said to Him, "Behold, I am going to the sons of Israel, and I will say to them, 'The Elohim of your fathers has sent me to you.' Now they may say to me, 'What is His name?'…," (Exodus 3:13). For some reason, Moses did not think it would be convincing enough to just say, *"Elohim sent me to deliver you."* He wanted to be prepared with a specific name for this Mighty One so they would know that Moses was coming on the highest authority, the One in whom they believed. It could have been that He wanted to give them a name that they would certainly identify as being the name of their el, Elohim, and, as a result, know that Moses could therefore be trusted.

Elohim, speaking from the burning bush, reveals to Moses this very personal, unique name by which He is to be forever known. This name does not appear in most of our English language Bibles, although it is in the Hebrew Scriptures. It is recorded in Exodus 3:15 that Elohim said, "Thus you shall say to the sons of Israel, the LORD, the God of your fathers, the God of Abraham, the God of Isaac, and the God of Jacob, has sent me to you." The correct translation from the Hebrew should be "Thus you shall say to the sons of Israel, YHWH, Elohim of your fathers, Elohim of Abraham, Elohim of Isaac, and Elohim of Jacob, has sent me to you." These four letters, YHWH, represent the consonants of the name of the Most High.

It was at this poignant moment in the history of the Hebrews as well as all of mankind that the Most High Elohim revealed His name for all to know Him. Hence, Moses was to take this name, YHWH, and go to the Israelites first and then to the Egyptians.

While on his way back to Egypt, Moses was joined by his brother,

Aaron, who YHWH said would be Moses' spokesman. When Moses and Aaron arrived in Egypt, they gathered the Israelite elders and told them that Elohim has heard and has answered their prayers.

> Then Moses and Aaron went and assembled all the elders of the sons of Israel; and Aaron spoke all the words which YHWH had spoken to Moses. He then performed the signs in the sight of the people. So the people believed; and when they heard that YHWH was concerned about the sons of Israel and that He had seen their affliction, then they bowed low and worshiped. (Exodus 4:29–31)

Following this, Moses and Aaron went to Pharaoh and asked for the release of the Israelite people so that they could go and worship Elohim, YHWH. Aaron spoke this very name to Pharaoh.

> And afterward Moses and Aaron came and said to Pharaoh, "Thus says YHWH, the Elohim of Israel, 'Let My people go that they may celebrate a feast to Me in the wilderness.' But Pharaoh said, "Who is YHWH that I should obey His voice to let Israel go? I do not know YHWH, and besides, I will not let Israel go." (Exodus 5:1–2)

The name of the Mighty One of Israel was made known to Pharaoh and the Egyptians. As a result, the Egyptians and other people also came to know who He is. This was Elohim's intended purpose, for He told Moses, "The Egyptians shall know that I am YHWH, when I stretch out My hand on Egypt and bring out the sons of Israel from their midst," (Exodus 7:5).

It was also during this period that the children of Israel came to really know Elohim by the fullness of His name. Prior to this, Elohim was known primarily to the Israelites and their forefathers as El Shaddai, which is traditionally translated as "God Almighty." It is believed by some that He had not revealed Himself by His proper name to even Abraham, Isaac, or Jacob (Exodus 6:2–3). However, the Scriptures do indicate that He was once known by His name. In the pre-flood period, during the time of Seth, the third son of Adam, men began to call upon YHWH by name (Genesis 4:26). Also, after the flood but before the encounter with Moses, we read that Abram (Abraham) built an altar and called on the name of YHWH (Genesis 12:8; 13:4). That is why we can draw the conclusion that this el who was from the beginning was never a nameless power. There is supporting evidence in scripture predating the time of Moses to suggest that His name was known by some people. Now, in Egypt during this time of deliverance, He seeks to make Himself known to the Israelites and, later, the Egyptians.

> "Say, therefore, to the sons of Israel, 'I am YHWH, and I will bring you out from under the burdens of the Egyptians, and I will deliver you from their bondage. I will also redeem you with an outstretched arm and with great judgments. 'Then I will take you for My people, and I will be your Elohim; and you shall know that I am YHWH your Elohim, who brought you out from under the burdens of the Egyptians. I will bring you to the land which I swore to give to Abraham, Isaac, and Jacob, and I will give it to you for a possession; I am YHWH.'" (Exodus 6:6–8)

Calling Him by His Name

As you read the Old Testament, you will notice that there are many times the name of Elohim is mentioned or referenced. The Bible writers write such phrases as "bless His holy name" (Psalm 145:21, 103:1), "call upon His name" (1 Chronicles 16:8; Psalm 105:1; Isaiah 12:4), "…in the name of YHWH" (Deuteronomy 18:7; Psalm 118:26, 124:8; Micah 4:5), "My name" (Exodus 3:15, 6:3, 9:16, 20:24, 23:21; Leviticus 19:12; Deuteronomy 18:19–20) (See Appendix B). All of these phrases were meant to draw attention to the name YHWH. Yet, despite all of these references to His name, the actual name is still unknown to many Bible readers. The Bibles we most often read, unfortunately, reference the name, but the actual name is not printed in the text. Instead, they include substitutions like "the LORD." To find the true name, readers most often will have to look not in the text of the Scriptures but elsewhere, such as in Bible encyclopedias, commentaries, and the notes written by Bible translators.

However, there are clues in most of our English language Bible translations—every occurrence of "the LORD," with "lord" written in capital letters, is where YHWH originally appeared in the Scriptures. There are over six thousand times this happens. Each time the name YHWH appears in the Scriptures, it is in the context of the Most High declaring His own name, an Israelite speaking to or about YHWH, or a non-Israelite speaking the name.

Elohim declares His name to the Israelite people on many occasions, and oftentimes it is done through His prophets. He spoke to Moses. He spoke through Moses to the people. He spoke to the prophets Elijah, Isaiah, Ezekiel, Jeremiah, etc. YHWH was not shy about using His name so that the people would know Him and the importance of His words and deeds (See Appendix C). He wanted His people with whom He had a covenant relationship to know Him in a very real, discernible way. They were to see YHWH as alive, powerful, capable, and merciful. They were to see Him as "set apart" or holy. By reminding them of His name repeatedly, YHWH was establishing an awareness of Him in the minds of the people. His acts, conquests, and words were to be clearly associated with Him by name and not just by El or Elohim. If His name was not tied to His mighty deeds and He was referred to in general terms, it would be easy for people to give or assign His glory to another. He was not some nebulous el. Although the term Elohim acknowledged Him as a majestic mighty power, it did not do Him justice. YHWH wanted to be identified and recognized for His own renown. He was, and is, YHWH, great and powerful.

While on top of Mount Sinai, as the Mighty One tells Moses the laws He has for the people, He begins by identifying Himself.

> "I am YHWH your Elohim, who brought you out of the land of Egypt, out of the house of slavery. You shall have no other elohim before Me. You shall not make for yourself an idol, or any likeness of what is in heaven above or on the earth beneath or in the water

under the earth. You shall not worship them or serve them; for I, YHWH your Elohim, am a jealous Elohim, visiting the iniquity of the fathers on the children, on the third and the fourth generations of those who hate Me, but showing lovingkindness to thousands, to those who love Me and keep My commandments. You shall not take the name of YHWH your Elohim in vain, for YHWH will not leave him unpunished who takes His name in vain." (Exodus 20:2–7)

There is no mistaking that YHWH wanted these people whom He delivered out of Egypt to know Him and not mistake Him for some other power worshiped by other nations. Without a doubt, there were other powers or idols. YHWH was well aware of this and the propensity of people to go after these different powers and idols. Therefore, for Him, it was imperative that He, YHWH, alone be worshiped and identified by His personal name by His chosen people. As a matter of fact, in the book of Leviticus alone, where YHWH tells Moses the laws the people are to obey, He said His own name 160 times.

After hearing all of the commandments and statutes that YHWH presented, the children of Israel assert that they would indeed do all that YHWH had commanded and pledge their allegiance to Him. "So Moses came and called the elders of the people, and set before them all these words which YHWH had commanded him. All the people answered together and said, 'All that YHWH has spoken we will do!' And Moses brought back the words of the people to YHWH" (Exodus 19:7–8). So, in their distress, they call out YHWH's name. In conversing about Him, they use His name. In their praise to Him, they sing His name: YHWH.

After the children of Israel were delivered from their Egyptian bondage, the news of YHWH spread. As the Israelites encountered various nations on their journey and during their forty years of wandering in the wilderness, these nations knew what this specific el, YHWH, had done for this people. These nations even spoke of YHWH by name (Numbers 22; Joshua 2:1–14, 9:1–11). The Bible speaks of people approaching the Israelites even after they had settled in the land of Canaan, the Promised Land, and mentioning YHWH by name (2 Kings 18:17ff). His name was by no means a secret to anyone—then.

Using the name of YHWH prevented any remote chance of confusing Him with another. Using YHWH's name also allowed the people to express His past actions as well as their expectations of Him and His honorable character without reciting a whole dissertation. His name said it all. Experience and time had allowed the people to know not just the possessor of that name but also all that that name encompassed. Not everyone who said His name initially respected YHWH, but for many who said the name with derision, YHWH proved Himself to be a mighty power that later commanded their respect (1 Kings 10:1–10; 2 Kings 19:5–7; 35–37).

The Four Letters

Today when we see the personal name of Elohim written in the English alphabet, we mostly see the four consonants Y-H-W-H. There are other variations of this (such as YHVH), but the most common is YHWH. That is today, but four thousand years ago when the name was written, it is believed that it was written like this and was read from right to left:

The majority of the Old Testament books were originally written in the Hebrew language; and it is believed that they were written using Ancient Hebrew script, including the name for the Mighty One of Israel. Of course, back when these books were written, the printing press was not invented and everything was handwritten. So the above example may be a good representation of what the Hebrew letters may have looked like as they were carved into various surfaces or written on papyrus or some other materials. Unfortunately, there are no known copies or artifacts of the Scriptures written in the Ancient Hebrew script from the period preceding the Israelites forced exile from the land they inherited. The twelve tribes of Israel lived in the Promised Land as one nation but later split into two kingdoms. The Northern Kingdom was the first to be exiled to Assyria 478 years after Moses died, and they were led into the land by Joshua. The Southern Kingdom was overtaken by the Babylonians some 136 years later and lived in exile for 70 years. Up until this Babylonian exile, it is believed that the first five books of the Bible known as the Books of the Law, or Torah, were written in Ancient Hebrew script along with other Israelite writings from that period.

The Old Testament books written during the Babylonian captivity, or thereafter, were written in the Aramaic language and not the Hebrew. For example, the books of Daniel, Nehemiah, and Ezra were written in the Aramiac language and letters. However, the books of Genesis, Exodus, Proverbs, etc. were all written in the Hebrew language and script. When the Israelites from the Southern Kingdom of Judea returned from their place of exile, Ezra the priest in 460 B.C.E. rewrote the scriptures using the Aramaic characters, or what is known as the Modern Hebrew script.

Most of the actual Hebrew manuscripts of these sacred books that survived and re-surfaced from those ancient days really are quite recent discoveries. Manuscripts of each of the books in the Old Testament, with the exception of the Book of Esther, were uncovered in the Dead Sea scrolls. The Dead Sea scrolls are the discovery of manuscripts and artifacts found in the caves near the Dead Sea. It is believed that these items belonged to a group of people known as the Essenes who lived at the end of the first century B.C.E. and into the first century C.E. The collection of the approximately 900 documents that make up the Dead Sea scrolls began to be discovered in 1947. These documents and partial manuscripts confirm that the Scriptures were, indeed, written in the Hebrew language in the first century. This had been suspected but never proved until the discovery of the Dead Sea scrolls.

Up until this breakthrough, the oldest available Hebrew manuscripts of the Scriptures dated to the seventh century C.E. The Dead Sea scroll manuscripts are from as early as the third century B.C.E. These relics were written in the Modern Hebrew script. Even with these finds, the Most High's name, YHWH, continued to be written in the Ancient Hebrew alphabet despite the rest of the text being printed in the Modern Hebrew script. See the illustration below of Psalm 119:59-64 found among the Dead Sea scrolls. The arrow points to the name YHWH. Notice that this script is completely different than the rest.

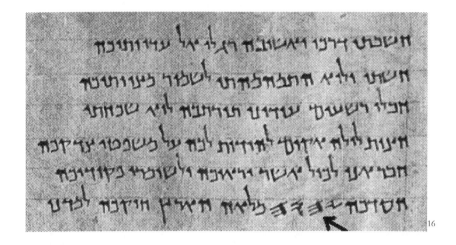

In the Modern Hebrew script, the name YHWH is written as יהוה not the handwritten letter-style shown in the Ancient Hebrew script. Reading from right to left as Hebrew is read, the letters are *yôd, hé, wāw,* and *hé*. (The *hé* is pronounced as the English word hey. The letter *wāw* is sometimes referred to as *or vāv* instead of *wāw*.) Translated into English, these four letters, commonly known as the Tetragrammaton, are the English letters YHWH. Tetragrammaton is a Greek word that literally means "word with four letters." This tetragrammaton, YHWH, is Elohim's name, the name of the el of the Israelites. Actually, the Tetragrammaton is found in the original Hebrew scriptural texts 6,823 times. The sheer frequency of its presence in the Scriptures is an indication of its importance. It is, therefore, imperative that we come to terms with this name and give it proper respect—that is, at the minimum, acknowledgement.

There is No "J"

Now, one thing worth noting is that the name Jehovah cannot be the name for the Almighty. That is for good reason. The ancient Hebrew language did not include the letter "J." So, it would have been highly improbable that Elohim would have told Moses His name was one that began with the letter "J" or its sound if that was not a sound that was used during that time period. It is believed that the letter "J" did not come into full existence until somewhere around the 17th century when it was used as a variant of the letter "I." It was at this point that the letter had its own sound whereas before it was pronounced as the letters "I" or "Y." The "J" was the last letter to be added to the Roman alphabet and one of the least used.

English is one of the few languages that pronounce the "J" with the hard sound as in the word *jam*. Most other languages continue to pronounce it as if it was an "I" and give it a "Y" sound. As an example, the English word Judea had once been spelled out as Iudea with the letter "I" instead of "J," which we are now accustomed to seeing. Notice the difference below in the writing of the King James Version (1611/1769) and the Geneva Bible written in 1599. (Italics added for emphasis.)

King James Version 1611/1769	Geneva Bible 1599
Acts 11:1 And the apostles and brethren that were in *Judaea* heard that the Gentiles had also received the word of God.	**Acts 11:1** Nowe the Apostles and the brethren that were in *Iudea,* heard, that the Gentiles had also receiued the worde of God.

Since the letter "J" is not a valid letter or sound in the ancient Hebrew language and script, then there is no way to retrace this name Jehovah back to the Tetragrammaton, YHWH or its Hebrew equivalent. As it pertains to the name Jehovah, you only have three-fourths of the Tetragrammaton "_HVH" since the letter "J", or its sound equivalent, was not in existence. Given this, we can concede that there was a serious attempt made to get to the Hebrew name. Clearly, the people who originally proposed that Jehovah was the name of the Most High made some effort to give us a pronunciation of the Hebrew as they understood it at that time. Unfortunately, the first letter is off. Even if there is no certainty on the vowels to use for the name, it would be better for those who are trying to honor His name to be, at least, as consistent as possible with the Hebrew letters we do know. Hence, it would be appropriate to drop the "J" and replace it with a "Y."

Pronunciation

The four consonants Y-H-W-H give very little clue as to how the name is to be pronounced. There are four things that should be known when trying to determine the correct pronunciation of YHWH. First, the pronunciation of the consonants is not as clear-cut as one would expect. For example, the letter *wāw* or *vāv* is either pronounced as a "W" and a "V" depending on the individual speaker's understanding, training, or background. For example, people from European descent may tend to pronounce it as a "V." For this reason, you will sometimes see the Tetragrammaton as YHVH instead of YHWH. The most widely accepted pronunciation for YHWH is Yahweh (sounds like Yah-way). If the *vāv* is assumed to be correct by the speaker, then instead of saying Yahweh, the speaker would say Yahveh (sounds like Yah-veigh). Also, regarding pronunciation of the consonants, the *hé* can be pronounced as an "H" as in the word *hat*. However, some people pronounce the first *hé* in YHWH that ends the first syllable as if it was a hard "CH." When they say the name, it may sound like "Yak-way" or "Yak-vey."

In determining the pronunciation, the second thing to consider is that there are some people who lean to a three-syllable word as opposed to the two-syllable rendering discussed thus far. The three-syllable pronunciation of YHWH generally strengthens or doubles the first *hé*. Strengthening certain consonants is sometimes done in Hebrew. Rather than write a letter twice as we do in English, in Hebrew it is written one time. And, for most letters, there is a specific marking that makes the reader aware that a particular letter should be doubled. However, these markings known as dagesh forte do not occur in the letter *hé*. Yet those who support the three-syllable pronunciations assert that the *hé* has been strengthened; this not only closes the first syllable but also begins the second syllable. For this reason, we have some people who pronounce YHWH as Yeh–ho-wah, Yah-ho-weh, Yah-ho-vah, or some variation of this. The three-syllable pronunciation is also done without the doubling of the hé. Those who do this usually put a vowel, either an *o* or *u*, between the first and last syllables. Some have come to this pronunciation based on the premise that the Hebrew letters in the Tetragrammaton are their own vowels and that applying those vowel sounds results in YHWH being pronounced YeHoWaH or YaHoWaH.[17]

The third thing to keep in mind is that any vowels placed between these consonants are mere educated guesses. The ancient Hebrew language did not include vowels in the writing of texts. When the Old Testament Scriptures were written, the original text consisted of consonants only. Later, as the Scriptures were rewritten in the Middle Ages by scribes[18] known as the Masoretes, vowels were added (whether vowels were used prior to this is a matter of debate). The vowels that were added to the four Hebrew consonants of the Tetragrammaton were inserted as they did with any other Hebrew word. The Masoretes added vowels based on the way the word or name was commonly pronounced.

The Hebrew vowels are markings that consist of dots and tittles that are known as points and are usually found beneath the Hebrew consonant. It should be noted, first of all, that there is much disagreement about the correct vowel points added to known consonants. In the case of YHWH, the Hebrew vowel points on the Tetragrammaton can look like the following, which will add a soft, short "a" or "e" sound after the Y or *yôd* and a long "a" sound after the W or *wāw*:

Therefore, if spelling the word out based on how it sounds, known as transliteration, the word would look like this:

Yahwah

Some say that the vowel points used in the name YHWH are taken from the vowels used in the word Adonai, the Hebrew word for "lord" or "master." "In written texts, the vowels of Adonai were combined with the consonants of YHWH to remind readers to pronounce Adonai instead of Yahweh."[19] You see, at a point in the history of the Israelites, the people were prohibited (by man, not Elohim) from speaking the name YHWH. The religious leaders had taken on a new commitment to honoring the Almighty and their covenant relationship with Him. After many years of not serving YHWH as He commanded but serving the elohim of other nations, the Israelites felt the consequences of their disobedience. For YHWH allowed another country, Babylon, to overtake and remove them from their land. They remained in captivity for 70 years and experienced what it was like to not have YHWH's favor. When the Israelites returned from their captivity, they did so committed to being faithful to YHWH like never before.

This new commitment came with some interpretations and practices of the Torah that were different than the original intent. The religious leaders turned the practice of serving YHWH into a religion. This was never meant to be. They imposed practices that forced limits on the people's freedoms just to avoid transgressing what they thought to be YHWH's law. One such limit was on speaking the Most High's name. Initially, the prohibition applied to the common people. Later, the ban extended to the priests who were limited to saying the name only when pronouncing a blessing. Then, only the high priest was allowed to speak the name aloud. The end result was that the audible pronunciation of the name, YHWH, was no longer prominent in the lives and worship of the Israelites. When the people wanted to speak the name, they had to use an acceptable substitute instead such as "Ha Shem," which in translation means "*The Name.*" Or, they would say "Adonai," which was the most common substitute used. So, if a person was reading scripture and came across the name YHWH in the text, the person would avoid speaking the name and say Adonai instead. This practice of not saying the name went on for centuries and was even a custom during the time of the Messiah and thereafter.

Now, during the period when the Masoretes were copying the Tanakh, what we call the Old Testament scriptures, they attempted to copy the text word for word. When they came to the Most High's name, instead of just putting the Hebrew letters *yôd, hé, wāw,* and *hé,* which no one read aloud anymore, they wrote those four letters but added under it the letters for the word Adonai. For example, in Psalm 23:1, in Hebrew it would have been written:

$$\text{יְהוָה רֹעִי לֹא אֶחְסָר}$$
$$\text{אֲדוֹן}$$

Reading from right to left, the first word in the top line is YHWH, which would render the verse as *YHWH is my shepherd.* However, because the people were prohibited from actually saying YHWH, the word Adonai is found under it as a reminder for them to say Adonai instead of YHWH. Today, of course, many of us have always read it as *The Lord (Adonai) is my shepherd.* We never knew that the Psalmist was declaring *YHWH is my shepherd.*

Some believe that only the vowel points for Adonai were added instead of writing the full word for Adonai below YHWH. Therefore, it is believed that these vowel points were placed under the Tetragrammaton to indicate the correct pronunciation of YHWH. However, this very well may not be the case, but such vowel points may merely have been the Masoretes way of reminding people to say Adonai when they came across the name YHWH in the readings. Possibly, later when the vowel points were added to the Hebrew text, it was then that the vowels for Adonai remained with YHWH. Thereby, the vowels for YHWH were established.

Another plausible theory regarding the pronunciation of the name centers around two Hebrew verbs. It is believed that these two verbs are the root of each of the two syllables of the name YHWH. Further, these two verbs describe who Elohim is. His name has significant meaning when each of these syllables is viewed from the context of the verbs from which they stem.

When Moses asked the Most High what should he say to the children of Israel when they ask him for the name of the Mighty One who sent him to deliver them, this was the response:

> Elohim said to Moses, "I AM WHO I AM"; and He said, "Thus you shall say to the sons of Israel, 'I AM has sent me to you.'" (Exodus 3:14)

The Hebrew for *"I AM WHO I AM"* is transliterated "Ehyeh-Asher-Ehyeh." The word *Ehyeh* is the first person singular of the Hebrew verb HaYaH, which is the verb "to be." The letters of this verb is simply hé, yôd, and hé, which is pronounced as ha-yah. The *Yah* in Yahwah comes from *hayah*. Yah is actually a shortened, poetic version of YHWH's name that is found in the Hebrew text of the Scriptures, most often in the book of Psalm. Many people choose to call YHWH *Yah* instead of His full name. Now, the second part of the name comes from the Hebrew verb HaWaH, which is the verb "to become." The Hebrew letters of HaWaH, *hé*, *wāw*, and *hé*, is pronounced as *ha-wah* in transliteration. You may have already noticed that this verb includes the *wāw* and *hé* found in the last part of the name YHWH.

Let's look at these two verbs and see not just how the name YHWH may derive from them but also its meaning.

$$\text{יְהוָה רֹעִי לֹא אֶחְסָר}$$
$$\text{אָדוֹן}$$

Now, the fourth and final point to consider concerning the pronunciation of the name YHWH is that no one alive today may really know definitively how YHWH is correctly pronounced. We all just do the best we can based on what we do know. And what we do know is that His name, יהוה, is by no means pronounced "the LORD" as we have, in the English-speaking world, come to acknowledge it over the centuries.

Chapter Five:
His Name Was Blotted Out

THE BIBLICAL ACCOUNT OF THE ISRAELITES' FORTY-YEAR journey from Egypt to the Land of Promise illustrates the prominent role that YHWH had in this. All of the many exploits of YHWH on behalf of the Israelites—including His provisions, protection, deliverance, fighting, and conquering—resulted in the other peoples or nations recognizing this mighty power. Some of these people became acquainted with His name and either came to respect Him or challenge Him. The children of Israel were taught His name but, at times, forgot to respect and fear Him. Forgetting to respect and fear Him always came with a price. However, even with the cost of unfaithfulness, time after time, the children of Israel continued to forget Him.

While on their journey to Canaan, Moses went alone to the top of the mountain to speak to YHWH. He had been gone for what seemed to be a long time; therefore, the people assumed that Moses may have died on Mount Sinai. The Israelites then began to pester Aaron, Moses' brother, to give them an idol to worship. So, he melded gold and fashioned it into a golden calf that they began to worship as their mighty one. This act got the attention of YHWH so much so that He interrupted His conversation with Moses.

> Then YHWH spoke to Moses, "Go down at once, for your people, whom you brought up from the land of Egypt, have corrupted themselves. They have quickly turned aside from the way which I commanded them. They have made for themselves a molten calf, and have worshiped it and have sacrificed to it and said, 'This is your elohim, O Israel, who brought you up from the land of Egypt!'" (Exodus 32:7–8)

Later, while in the wilderness near Shittim, the children of Israel turned their hearts from YHWH and began to worship the el of the people of Moab known as Baal Peor. Sacrificing and bowing down to foreign elohim began when the Israelites married or took Moabite women as lovers. These women influenced the men to adopt their customs and become unfaithful to YHWH. "So Israel joined themselves to Baal of Peor, and YHWH was angry against Israel. YHWH said to Moses, 'Take all the leaders of the people and execute them in broad daylight before YHWH, so that the fierce anger of YHWH may turn away from Israel'" (Numbers 25:3–4). As a result, 24,000 people died in a plague because they failed to remember their covenant with YHWH and forgot to respect and fear Him (Numbers 25:9).

Even after this event and all that they had experienced with YHWH, the people who finally possessed the Promised Land failed to prepare their own children to maintain a commitment to YHWH. They did not teach them who He even was. "All that generation also were gathered to their fathers; and there arose another generation after them who did not know YHWH, nor yet the work which He had done for Israel," (Judges 2:10).

From time to time throughout the biblical accounts of the Israelites' history, we are reminded that they indeed had forgotten YHWH. They seemed to always be encased in a vicious cycle of knowing YHWH and then forgetting Him. They would commit to YHWH and then were led astray into the worship of other elohim and idols. Then as their lives went into a tailspin, a judge or a prophet would help them to return to YHWH. It would seem that the Torah should have been a good tool to help them remember YHWH and all He had done for them. Even if the people did not have a personal knowledge of YHWH, the written Scriptures did speak of Him by name. But they were not always committed to having the Scriptures read as they were supposed to. When the kingdom was split into two, the challenge to remember YHWH became even greater for those in the Northern Kingdom of Israel. The temple was in the Southern Kingdom, where they no longer went as required by the Father three times a year (Deuteronomy 16:16).

Despite this, there was a strong oral tradition that existed in their culture that kept information alive from generation to generation. There were prophets who spoke for Him as well as priests and Levites who certainly knew Him. So, the name YHWH was not completely lost to them. However, there was a progression of events that led to blotting out His name from the people's minds as well as from the Scriptures.

Following the Babylonian Exile

As a result of their failure to obey YHWH and refusal to turn from serving idols, He punished Judah, the Southern Kingdom. Years earlier, the Northern Kingdom of Israel was overtaken and led away by the Assyrians because of their unfaithfulness to YHWH. Despite seeing this and hearing the warnings from the prophets, their brothers to the south continued in their wickedness before the Almighty. So, YHWH sent the Babylonians to overthrow the inhabitants of Judah from their land. This was the beginning of the Babylonian exile.

In 586 B.C.E., the Israelites referred to as Judeans (really, Yehudim, as the letter "J" did not exist), who were living in the Kingdom of Judah, were taken into captivity. While in Babylon and exposed to a totally different culture, the people learned the Aramaic language, the language of their captors. The prophets Ezra, Nehemiah, and Daniel wrote the Old Testament books attributed to each of them in the Aramaic language. Ezra, the prophet, later rewrote the Scriptures after his return to Jerusalem. It is believed that he replaced the Old Hebrew characters with the Aramaic letters.

As early as the sixth century B.C.E., the Greek culture had begun to spread and, with it, the Greek language. This spreading of the Greek culture to areas outside of Greece is referred to as Hellenization. By the time the Israelites had begun their return from exile in 456 B.C.E., the Greek culture had already begun to take root. In less than 150 years, most people in Judea, the area where the Israelites returned, spoke Aramaic, and most of the tradespeople in that area spoke Greek. The more aristocratic Hebrew Israelites continued to speak their native language of Hebrew in addition to Greek.

When the Babylonian exile was over, some Israelites did not return to Judea but continued to live in Babylon, Egypt, and other parts of the world. "These international Jews (the Diaspora) prospered in a vital, Hellenized Judaism in cities like Alexandria."[20] During this Hellenistic period in which Alexander the Great, leader of the Greek Empire, expanded his empire and the Greek influence, the Hebrew worship of YHWH underwent some challenges. No longer were most Israelites able to speak or read their own language, Hebrew. There were Greek-speaking Israelites who did not have the experience of living in the culture of their own people. These were people who you might classify as being displaced. With the Hebrew Scriptures written only in Hebrew and Aramaic, this posed a problem for the Israelites who wanted to study their holy book. Also, it made it impossible for interested non-Israelites to read for themselves the words in the Hebrew Scriptures.

The Septuagint

During his political reign, Alexander the Great, out of curiosity about the Israelites and their beliefs, sought to know more about them. Therefore, he wanted to read their most sacred book. It was then that the Tanakh, or what we call today the Old Testament, was translated into Greek. He commissioned a committee of Hebrew scholars to translate the Hebrew Scriptures into Greek. The outcome of this committee resulted in the Greek translation commonly known as the

Septuagint or LXX, meaning 70, possibly referring to the 72 men who composed the document.

There seems to be evidence that the earlier versions of the Septuagint, although written in Greek, continued to have YHWH's name written in the ancient Hebrew letters. In true translations, the names of individuals which are proper nouns do not change even though other words are translatable. YHWH is still YHWH regardless of what language is used. Therefore, the early Septuagint writings had the Greek text, but the Most High's name, YHWH, continued to appear in the text in the Hebrew letters.

During this period, even though the YHWH's name was still written in their Scriptures, the Israelites would not read the name aloud. This prohibition on speaking the name occurred prior to the Septuagint. You see, it was when the Judeans returned from their Babylonian exile that the practice started among these Israelites of not saying YHWH's name out loud. "The postexilic Jewish practice of substituting *ªdōnāy* (or *ʾᵉlōhîm*) for *Yahweh* in the public reading or reciting of the scriptures may have risen from Leviticus 24:16, interpreted (erroneously) to mean that the simple utterance of the sacred Tetragrammaton was a capital offense, or from the fear that to pronounce the divine name would be to reduce God to the status of a pagan deity who was addressed by a personal name."[21] Centuries passed and the practice or tradition of not saying the name of the Most High continued. Even Flavius Josephus, a well-known and respected first-century Hebrew historian who wrote extensively about the history of his people, makes mention of the prohibition of using the Most High's name. In his writings known as *The Works of Josephus* in which he writes what has been called the *Antiquities of the Jews*, he recounts the Exodus story. It is here that he says that Elohim declared His name but it is unlawful for him to say it.

> Whereupon God declared to him his holy name, which had never been revealed to men before; concerning which it is not lawful for me to say anymore... [22]

Josephus reported what was the current custom of his time. The priests forbade people to utter the name YHWH, and, now, they had scriptures to back them up—the Greek translation of the Scriptures, that is. Actually, the original Hebrew Scriptures did not prohibit the speaking of the name YHWH. This was imposed by the traditions of the leaders and not the law of the Most High. For the Hebrews who only read the Septuagint, they relied on a translation that did not always accurately reflect the original writings as found in the Hebrew texts. The Septuagint translation of text actually forbade the people from saying YHWH's name out loud. Saying the name, in the Septuagint translation of Torah, would be worthy of death. Leviticus 24:16 is one such verse. The English translation of this Septuagint verse reads as follows:

> And he that names the name of the Lord, let him die the death: let all the congregation of Israel stone him with stones; whether he be a stranger or a native, let him die for naming the name of the Lord. (Septuagint - Leviticus 24:16)

However, the English translation of the Hebrew version of the very same verse reads differently.

> Moreover, the one who blasphemes the name of the LORD shall surely be put to death; all the congregation shall certainly stone him. The alien as well as the native, when he blasphemes the Name, shall be put to death. (Hebrew - Leviticus 24:16)

The mistranslation of the Septuagint of the Hebrew word *naqab*, which means "to curse" or "to blaspheme" resulted in people becoming fearful of audibly reading or saying the name YHWH.

The only people who were permitted to speak His name were the priests when pronouncing a blessing and the High Priest on the Day of Atonement. As time passed, this "privilege" was reserved only for the High Priest on that one day of the year. The people did not read the name YHWH even when they saw it in the Scriptures. Over time as the Masoretes copied the Scriptures for people to read, they omitted YHWH's Hebrew name altogether from the texts and substituted it with the Greek word for "lord," *Kurios*. All evidences of the name of

YHWH were gone. So, the ancient scribes who had the task of copying the Scriptures were trying to be consistent with the current practices.

During the time the Messiah was on earth, the Septuagint (LLX) was the version of the sacred texts that was most available to people. For many of the common people, especially those not well educated in the Hebrew language, this is what they read or were exposed to in their synagogues. "The LXX was the Bible for most writers of the New Testament...The LXX became the Bible of the early Church Fathers, and therefore helped to mold dogma..."[23] Actually, Israelites (Judeans and other descendents of Israel) and the followers of the Messiah used the Septuagint up until the second century C.E.

Beyond the Septuagint

It was during the second century that the Judeans began to discontinue the use of the Greek Septuagint in favor of the Hebrew text. Among the reasons they no longer used this as their main text was that they realized that many of the ideas in the Hebrew texts were not adequately conveyed in the Septuagint. However, another strong motive for abandoning the Septuagint was that it was too closely associated with those who followed and believed in the Messiah, who were becoming a growing but unpopular sect from whom the traditional Judeans wanted to be disassociated. These Judeans went back to the Hebrew/Aramaic texts and left the Greek translations of the Scriptures to the sect that believed in the Messiah—who were, for the most part, called Christians. By this time, the majority of these believers were Gentiles. They continued to use the Septuagint at least until other translations, such as the Latin Vulgate, became available.

Although traditional Judeans returned to the Hebrew texts of the Scriptures, they did not return to the practice of saying or reading YHWH's name, for the prohibition continued. The name and its correct pronunciation were still known at this time by some of these Hebrews, and they passed this knowledge on to only a few select people who sought to know the name or who were thought to be worthy to be entrusted with it. However, as the years passed, the pronunciation was lost because it was rarely spoken and too few people knew how to say it. When those who knew died, the pronunciation passed with them.

The first Greek translation of the Scriptures carried the Hebrew name for Elohim. However, as copies of the Septuagint were made over the years, the name YHWH was replaced with the Greek term *Kurios*. For many of the Gentile believers in the Messiah, the name was never known. First of all, the name did not appear in the Scriptures that they had been reading. Their Scriptures had the Greek word for lord/master, κύριος or *Kurios* as it is transliterated, in the place of YHWH. Also, as the years passed and the community of those who followed the Messiah grew, most people did not even have the Scriptures to read for themselves. So it is little wonder that after the passing of years and, then, centuries that there was no mention of the Most High's name in writings or in speech. The people had come to just accept whatever the tradition was to reference Him.

From the Christian tradition, the name of the Almighty really played almost no prominence. The 66 books of the Old Testament and New Testament, as we refer to them today, became the canons composing what is now known as the Holy Bible. This compiled text of books was translated into the many different languages of the people around the 14th century C.E. In many of these translations, however, YHWH, the name of the Mighty One of Israel, is not in the text.

So, for hundreds of years, Elohim's name has not been known by those who claim to have a relationship with Him through the Messiah. His name is not, or is rarely, uttered in the course of Bible study or many Christian worship services even today. While His name is not included in most of our Bibles, most Bible publishers do explain in their translation notes that they have replaced the true name, YHWH, with the words *the LORD*. Unfortunately, very few people really take the time to read the publisher's notes or introductory notes in their Bibles. They want to get straight to the Scripture texts. So, despite this disclosure, readers are clueless that this switch has purposely taken place. Seldom, if ever, do their Christian pastors and teachers reference this section of the Bible. And, sadly, rarely do they put any real emphasis on using the Almighty's true name.

Many people dismiss the importance of knowing or using the

proper name of the Most High. It seems to hold no relevance to their faith as far as they know. Yet, due to oversight and ignorance, Christians and seekers of truth have been missing out on the benefits of knowing the true and living Elohim. So much of knowing Him and being true worshipers is tied to His set-apart name. For it is a most reverent name. It is full of power and promise. It is a name that man did not ascribe to the Almighty but a name that He, Himself, uses to identify Himself. These four letters, Y-H-W-H, speak volumes about the Mighty One, who not only created the world and all that is in it but, also, who has been seeking to establish a relationship with humankind with all of its faults and failures.

Chapter Six:
YHWH Is His Name Forever

Then Moses said to Elohim, "Behold, I am going to the sons of Israel, and I will say to them, 'The Elohim of your fathers has sent me to you.' Now they may say to me, 'What is His name?' What shall I say to them?" Elohim said to Moses, "I AM WHO I AM"; and He said, "Thus you shall say to the sons of Israel, 'I AM has sent me to you.'" Elohim, furthermore, said to Moses, "Thus you shall say to the sons of Israel, 'YHWH, the Elohim of your fathers, the Elohim of Abraham, the Elohim of Isaac, and the Elohim of Jacob, has sent me to you.' This is My name forever, and this is My memorial-name to all generations." (Exodus 3:13–15)

MOSES ASKED THE MOST HIGH ELOHIM TO let him know His name. And, the response from the Most High was "I AM THAT I AM," which is translated from the Hebrew in this way:

The first and last words are the same. It is the Hebrew verb "to be," first person singular, imperfect tense. This verb appears twice and is separated by a relative article that is translated as "who" or "that," in this particular context. So, a more literal translation of Elohim's response to Moses' inquiry about His name is "I will be who I will be." It is in the next verse that Elohim, for the first time, refers to His name. It is this verse that He says יְהֹוָה אֱלֹהֵי or YHWH Elohe, in transliteration. It appears as LORD God in most English Bible versions, though, for reasons that we have already discussed.

Notice that Elohim clearly states "this *is* My name forever." Another four thousand years may pass and His name will remain YHWH, not "the LORD" and not "God." YHWH is the only name of the Mighty One who established a covenant with Abraham, Isaac, Jacob, their physical descendents, and the other people who join in serving Him.

His Name Before Moses

YHWH was not always known by His personal name, at least according to some people's understanding of biblical accounts. However, there is a strong possibility that before the flood He was, indeed, known by this name. There are two incidences recorded in history, prior to the time of Moses, where the writer of Genesis indicated that a person or people "called on the name of YHWH." If one is to call upon the name of YHWH or the name of Elohim, then they would, in all likelihood, have to know the name by which they are calling. The first time that people actually called upon the name of YHWH was after Adam's third son, Seth, began to have children (Genesis 4:26). The assumption could be made that, prior to this time, the people of the earth did not proclaim YHWH's name.

Some of Seth's descendents had noteworthy relationships with YHWH. The Scriptures say that one such descendent was a man named Enoch. It is said that "Enoch walked with Elohim" (Genesis 5:22, 24), implying that he lived in a way that was pleasing to the Creator. Another descendent of Seth that found favor in YHWH's eyes was a man named Abram (whom we know as Abraham, the name later assigned by YHWH). Abram proved faithful when he followed YHWH to the land of Canaan, which was promised to his descendents. It was there that Abram found a spot to pitch his tent. Then, he built an altar to YHWH, and the Scriptures say he called on YHWH's name (Genesis 12:8).

Moses and the Name

Centuries later, when Abraham's descendents were in the land of Egypt, YHWH revealed His name to Moses during an encounter on a mountainside. Later, when Moses was in Egypt on his mission for YHWH and was a little disheartened by Pharaoh's response to letting the Israelites go, YHWH, again, told Moses His name.

> Elohim spoke further to Moses and said to him, "I am YHWH; and I appeared to Abraham, Isaac, and Jacob, as El Shaddai, but by My name, YHWH, I did not make Myself known to them." (Exodus 6:2–3)

In these verses, three points are made. First, YHWH confirmed to Moses His name. Second, He stated that when He appeared before Abraham, Isaac, and Jacob, He did so as El Shaddai. And third, He did not reveal Himself to the forefathers by His name, YHWH.[24]

Moses is believed to be the author of the first five books of the Scriptures. So, when we read these books, we should not be surprised to see the name YHWH occurring frequently. After all, this is the name by which Moses came to know the Almighty. This, also, is the very name that the Most High, personally, told Moses was His. On many occasions, He even declared this name to the people for them to know and reverence.

By: Iris A. Foreman

The Name and the Prophets

It is not only in the writings of Moses that the name YHWH is noted as being the name of the Almighty. There are also repeated occurrences in the books of the prophets as well. Some of the prophetic books mention the name YHWH more than others, but for the most part, there is no doubt that YHWH is the Mighty Power who speaks to the Israelites. If you examine the books of what is considered the former prophets (Joshua, Judges, Samuel, and Kings), you will find YHWH by His personal name directing, speaking, and leading the people as they conquer, enter into, and dwell in the land He promised to give them. Then, when you read the latter prophets (Amos, Hosea, Micah, Isaiah, Zephaniah, Nahum, Habakkuk, Jeremiah, Ezekiel, Obadiah, Joel, Jonah, Haggai, Zechariah, and Malachi), YHWH, by name, is represented.

These prophets spoke to the people what YHWH had given them to speak and quoted Him, making direct references in identifying His name. For example, the Prophet Isaiah records, "...I am YHWH; that is my name..." (Isaiah 42:8). Likewise, Jeremiah records, "...they shall know that my name is YHWH..." (Jeremiah 16:21).

The prophets remind the people that the name of their Elohim is YHWH. They communicated such reminders as, "YHWH of host is his name" or "YHWH is his name." It is this very name that the prophet Joel tells the people to call on for their deliverance. "And it will come about that whoever calls on the name of YHWH will be delivered..." (Joel 2:32). The name that Joel actually writes is YHWH not *the LORD,* as we have been led to believe. This is significant. For deliverance and salvation is not in *the LORD* but in YHWH. YHWH is quite specific throughout all of His messages He gave to His prophets for the people that He, YHWH, is the Mighty One and that they are to know and worship Him alone.

There is some debate about the time period when the prophet Joel wrote these words. Was it before or after the Babylonian exile? What we do know is that it was at this time that YHWH spoke through Joel about the time of destruction that was to be called *the Day of YHWH* or as our Bible say *the Day of the LORD.* This is a period when the Almighty's wrath will pour out on mankind because of all the wickedness. It will be a day of doom when the earth will react at the Almighty's direction, and darkness and gloom will terrorize man. Joel urges the inhabitants of the Kingdom of Judah to return to serving YHWH so that they can be spared. When His people repent, He will deliver them. He is their Elohim. Israel will be a great nation again because YHWH will deliver them. He will pour out His spirit upon them because they called upon His name, *YHWH*. Centuries later, the Son of Elohim, the Messiah, came proclaiming that the Kingdom of YHWH was at hand. He encouraged people, fellow Israelites, to repent and truly turn to YHWH. His message was not well received, and as a result, he was crucified. However, three days later, according to the Scriptures, YHWH resurrected the Messiah from the dead. Following his resurrection, the Messiah ascended to heaven, leaving his disciples to spread the good news.

"And it shall be that everyone who calls on the name of YHWH will be saved" (Acts 2:21). It was one of his closest disciples, Peter, who quoted these very words from the prophet Joel. Remember that the practice at that time was to substitute another word for YHWH, and Adonai was often the substitute used. If Peter had been taught the Scriptures from the Greek Septuagint, then it is very likely he himself may have read Adonai or even Kurios instead of saying YHWH, yet all of the time meaning YHWH. Remember that the practice at that time was to substitute another word for YHWH, and *Adonai* was often the substitute used. If Peter was taught the Scriptures from the Greek Septuagint, then it is very likely he himself may have read *Adonai* or even *Kurios*.

His Name After the Resurrection

Today when we read the text in the book of Acts in our English translations, we see *"And it shall be that everyone who calls on the name of the LORD will be saved."* In many Christian circles, the assumption is that Peter was saying that one must call on the name of the Messiah to be saved. It is not clear to many whom the term *Lord* is referring to, but because the Christian doctrine teaches that the Messiah is the savior, then it is believed that this verse is speaking of him. Matthew Henry writes in his commentary on this verse, "The signal preservation of the Lord's people is here promised (v21): Whosoever shall call upon the name of the Lord Jesus shall be saved."[25] I am inclined to believe that Peter, being a Hebrew and a descendent of Israel, was referring to YHWH even if he did not say His name when quoting this particular verse. It would be unseemly for Peter to misquote the verse and say the Greek or Hebrew word for Lord implying the Messiah. His audience on that day was composed of Israelites, who knew that verse or had some knowledge that the salvation of Israel historically had been YHWH and they would have expected it to be Him in the future howbeit through His Messiah.

To misquote the prophet Joel's words and imply that a man and not YHWH was to be the salvation of Israel probably would have resulted in a major disturbance in this crowd of Hebrews. The city was overflowing with Israelites who had journeyed to Jerusalem for the Feast of the Harvest of the First Fruits (also called the Feast of Weeks or Pentecost).[26] Peter's audience were people like him—people who worshiped and feared YHWH and sought to be obedient to the Torah, Elohim's laws. It would have been almost suicidal for Peter to address this crowd by misquoting or giving a variant interpretation of their Scriptures. What Peter spoke was a verse that was familiar to them, the Scriptures that were being fulfilled before their very eyes. In the Messiah's teaching and living, he pointed to YHWH. So did Peter in his message and exhortation. He pointed to YHWH with the Messiah being the promise of the Elohim of Israel. The fact that Peter and the other disciples recognized the Messiah for who he was did not stop them from being Hebrew Israelites who worshiped YHWH. "And it shall be that everyone who calls on the name of YHWH will be saved" (Acts 2:21). They now were able to worship YHWH in the truth that the Messiah gave them.

Chapter Seven:
"The Lord" Cannot Help Us

I<small>F</small> YHWH IS THE NAME BY WHICH salvation comes, why is it that
His actual name is not known by the people who say they are His
worshipers? If His name is important, why have our pastors and teachers
not told us? These are questions I had to ask myself. And I am sure many
other people are asking the same questions. Too often, we look to what
others have written in the past and what our religious leaders have taught
us regarding matters of faith to determine what is relevant or not. If none
of our contemporary leaders are putting emphasis on knowing the name
of the one they say they serve, then we automatically assume that it is not
important for our salvation and our relationship with Him. If we search the
Christian writings from past Christian theologians and the Early Church
Fathers and see no emphasis on this subject, then we would also conclude
that the name of the Creator of the heavens and earth holds no relevance
to His worshipers. Unfortunately, these assumptions and conclusions
regarding minimizing His name are faulty. Back in the latter part of the
seventh century B.C.E. and the beginning of the sixth century B.C.E., the
prophet Jeremiah prophesied that this would happen. To better understand
this, we must first understand what prophecy has said regarding this.

The Prophecies

How did the people forget the name YHWH as the name of the Most High? The answer is found in the book of Jeremiah. YHWH told Jeremiah that there will be false prophets who will not speak for Him—that is, speak His words. These false prophets will tell their own imaginations or dreams to the people. "I have heard what the prophets said, that prophesy lies in my name, saying, 'I have dreamed, I have dreamed'" (Jeremiah 23:25).

You see, these people, as YHWH foretold, will speak of dreams that they contrived themselves and were not given to them by Elohim, despite their pronouncement that the message was from Him. They will seek to mislead the people for their own personal gain, to appease the authorities, or for some other reason. Therefore, they will act without compunction to spread what is false and attribute it to YHWH. What we do know is that their lies, regarding the so-called dreams, will not please YHWH.

It is because of these lying prophets that YHWH said that His name would be forgotten. "...Is there *anything* in the hearts of the prophets who prophesy falsehood, even *these* prophets of the deception of their own heart, who intend to make My people forget My name by their dreams which they relate to one another, just as their fathers forgot My name because of Baal?" (Jeremiah 23:26–27). Basically, YHWH is saying that what is in the hearts of these so-called prophets is deceit; and this deceit will result in the people of YHWH forgetting His name. It is bad enough that they will forget their Elohim's name and, thereby, forget YHWH; but they will forget His name because they will be caught up in worshiping Baal. So, instead of remembering Elohim, whom they and their fathers knew as YHWH, they will no longer know, recognize, or acknowledge the name YHWH. Rather, they will think that their Elohim's name was Baal, which really is a translation for the word *lord*.

Prophecies Fulfilled

This is where we are today. The vast majority of people do not know YHWH as the name of the Elohim of Abraham, Isaac, and Jacob. This is because some prophet or prophets, years and years ago, caused the people to stop reading and speaking the name aloud. However, we may say that the verse in Jeremiah 23 is not fully fulfilled because we have not forgotten the Most High's name for "Baal." We are only guilty of using the words *the* LORD instead of YHWH. You may say that we certainly have not desecrated His memory by assigning Him the name Baal.

Well, what or who is Baal, then? We have been taught that Baal is a false god that the pagan nations used to worship back during the times of the Old Testament. We know the story of the prophet Elijah confronting the 450 prophets of Baal during the reign of King Ahab and his infamous wife Jezebel (1 Kings 18). We have heard of the various times that Israel turned from serving YHWH to worshiping the baals of the nations around them, even after they were warned not to do so (Numbers 25:1–9, Judges 2:8-15, 2 Kings 17:6–16).

Many of us would say that we have not replaced YHWH's name for Baal. Yet in reality our forefathers did and we, too, have done so as a result of our generation not knowing His name.

If you look at any Bible dictionary or encyclopedia, you will see that Baal means "lord." Easton's Bible Dictionary states the following:

> **382 Baal**, lord. (1.) The name appropriated to the principal male god of the Phoenicians. It is found in several places in the plural BAALIM…The sun-god, under the general title of Baal, or "lord," was the chief object of worship of the Canaanites. Each locality had its special Baal, and the various local Baals were summed up under the name of Baalim, or "lords."[27]

There were many baals in the Bible. So, often when there is a reference to a baal that is worshiped by the people, it is of an idol or false *power*, a master that the people serve that is not YHWH. However, in the book of Hosea, there is reference to the people calling YHWH "Baali," meaning "my lord," when they should have been calling Him

'Ishi,' which means "my husband" (Hosea 2:16). Hosea spoke to the people during a period when they were being unfaithful to YHWH by going after other elohim, or baals. They were so deep in their unfaithfulness that they had even resorted to calling YHWH Baali, looking at Him as if He were like the baals or lords that the other peoples served.

Tradition and practice have us referring to the Elohim of Abraham, Issac, and Jacob as *the LORD*. His name, YHWH, has, indeed, been forgotten for the title *Lord* (Baal). Instead of calling YHWH by His name, which He wanted to be known by, we have replaced it. Let's look at what the committee of translators of New Revised Standard Version of The Holy Bible says about the reason this committee continued the practice of not disclosing the name of YHWH in scripture. Bruce M. Metzger writes:

> …The use of any proper name for the one and only God, as though there were other gods from whom the true God had to be distinguished, began to be discontinued in Judaism before the Christian era and is inappropriate for the universal faith of the Christian Church.[28]

According to Metzger, the sacred name was not only being discontinued to be spoken by the Hebrews, Elohim's chosen people, but it was determined that this name was found inappropriate for the "universal faith of the Christian Church." Unfortunately, Metzger does not expound on why using YHWH is "inappropriate." One can only surmise that this is all part of the grand scheme of the deceit spoken of by the prophet Jeremiah.

Rather than speculate why identifying the Elohim of the Bible as YHWH would not have been appropriate, I will leave that to the reader to draw his or her own conclusions. Whatever the underlying purpose of this deception, for the most part, YHWH's name has been removed from both our sacred texts and our minds for over two thousand years.

Chapter Eight:
The Messiah Made
His Name Known

As the approached the hour of his crucifixion in which he would endure inhumanity for humanity's sake, the Messiah prayed to the Heavenly Father for himself, his followers, and those who were yet to follow him. He spoke of the eternal life that he, the Messiah, was to give to those whom Elohim had given him.

> ...Father, the hour has come; glorify Your Son, that the Son may glorify You, even as You gave Him authority over all flesh, that to all whom You have given Him, He may give eternal life. This is eternal life, that they may know You, the only true God, and Jesus Christ whom You have sent. (John 17:1–3)

The Messiah's mission was to fulfill YHWH's purpose, which was to benefit both human beings and the Most High. On one hand, mankind benefited from the Messiah's work by having access to eternal life, which was forfeited by Adam. On the other hand, YHWH benefited because His creation would come to know Him. The Messiah's mission brought people into a relationship with YHWH that could only come from truly knowing Elohim. Knowing YHWH meant acknowledging Him as the only one and true Elohim, the true power and might, and worshiping Him as creator and ruler over all. Also, knowing YHWH meant knowing and accepting His righteousness and rejecting wickedness. It meant knowing His mighty acts, even the Messiah whom He sent to bring us to Him.

YHWH Before the Coming of the Messiah

Going back to the beginning, the first man, Adam, fellowshipped with the Creator. Unfortunately, Adam sinned and caused mankind's fall from grace. As we know, the earth later ran rampant with wickedness, so Elohim flooded the earth, sparing only Noah, his family, and some animals. YHWH sought to give mankind a new start through this righteous man. Later, YHWH established a covenant with Abraham, a descendent of Noah's son, Shem, promising to be his Elohim and give him a great family of descendents whom He would bless. Elohim kept His word and blessed the descendants of Abraham, but time and time again, they were hot and cold in their worship and obedience to Him. The Most High desired to have Abraham's descendents worship Him only and, ultimately, become a people who would lead all mankind to Him.

When the Israelites first took possession of the land that YHWH promised Abraham, Israel was a united kingdom—that is, all twelve tribes were together under one ruler. They lived in twelve territories allotted to them based on the twelve Israelite families, but they existed as a single nation with a single judge to rule over them. Later, when they begged for it, they had a single king—Saul, followed by David, and then Solomon, King David's son. The Israelites still had the tabernacle, which was constructed during the time of Moses that had the Ark of the Covenant, which represented YHWH's presence with them. This was later replaced with the permanent temple that King Solomon built for YHWH in Jerusalem. This temple was sanctioned by YHWH as the only place for the people to make their sacrifices, give offerings, and inquire of Him.

Things changed, however, after the death of King Solomon. When his son, King Rehoboam, reigned after his death, he burdened the people even more so than did King Solomon. It was then that ten tribes decided to separate and form their own kingdom. Jerusalem, where the temple and the priests were, was now in what was considered the Southern Kingdom or Judah, still under the rule of King Rehoboam. The descendents of King David continued to rule over this kingdom as long as the people had kings, for YHWH had promised David he would always have a son on the throne. The other ten tribes that withdrew formed the Northern Kingdom, or what was simply called Israel. Rivalry and conflict arose between the two Israelite kingdoms. Jeroboam, the first ruler of the Northern Kingdom at the time of the succession, built two golden calves for the people to worship as the powers that brought them out of Egypt, one in Bethel and the other in Dan (1 Kings 12). Hence, the people in the Kingdom of Israel (Northern Kingdom) became idol worshipers and turned away from YHWH. Their failure to obey the laws of YHWH incurred the Almighty's wrath. The Assyrian Empire eventually invaded the Northern Kingdom and led the Israelites away captive. These ten tribes of Israel, who were a part of this Assyrian exile, never returned to Israel as a group and were scattered among the nations.

The Southern Kingdom of Judah also began to worship idols and the mighty ones of the other nations despite having YHWH's temple and His priests in their midst. The history of this kingdom shows a people who waxed hot and cold in regards to their relationship with their Elohim. It was their failure to remain faithful to YHWH that resulted in their eventual exile to Babylon. Their Babylonian captivity lasted only seventy years, but it was long enough to make them remember YHWH, whom they had previously forsaken. When their captivity ended, they returned to Jerusalem with a renewed determination and commitment to YHWH.

Yet in all of this, YHWH still desired to be known by His people.

They forgot YHWH and, over time, even His name; but YHWH did not forget them.

During the approximate five hundred years leading to the birth of the Messiah, the Jerusalem that the exiles from the Babylonian captivity returned to and rebuilt suffered in many ways. By the time the Messiah was born, it had long since stop being an Israelite nation or even the once great Kingdom of Judah. This Promised Land was a land that others wanted to possess. Within that 500-year period, the Greek and the Roman empires fought each other on various occasions, and each periodically ruled this land. The Israelites watched their land, culture, and temple suffer in the upheaval. Acculturation was frequently forced upon the people. Rather than caving in and being annihilated as a people and culture, there existed a remnant of the Israelites who held their ground and still called on YHWH to come to their defense. They looked for the deliverer that YHWH had promised. They looked for the Anointed One, the Messiah.

The Messiah and the Name

The Messiah came. And he had great compassion for the people because they were lost. The book of Mark records it this way:

> When Jesus went ashore, He saw a large crowd, and He felt compassion for them because they were like sheep without a shepherd; and He began to teach them many things. (Mark 6:34)

The Messiah came to deliver them, but not in the manner that they had expected. First, He had to deliver them from their traditions and their misunderstandings of the Scriptures—for example, their refusal to speak the true name of YHWH. The Messiah had to show the people YHWH as He truly is and not as He had been presented to them through their traditions.

Reading the different accounts of the Messiah's ministry, in the first four books of the New Testament, it shows him correcting the religious practices and thoughts of the people and, most of all, pointing them to a true worship of Elohim. The Messiah taught that in order to worship or serve YHWH, people must know Him. When we look at the Messiah's prayer to YHWH on the night that he was betrayed in the garden, we see the goal of his ministry. "This is eternal life, that they may know You, the only true God, and Jesus Christ whom You have sent" (John 17.3). Knowing YHWH as the true power is just as integral to having eternal life as knowing the Messiah. Based on the Messiah's own words, the Most High's name was fundamental in the Messiah's mission. He saw that part of his mission was to make YHWH's name known. He refers to YHWH's name no fewer than five times during this prayer.

> I have manifested Your **name** to the men whom You gave Me out of the world; they were Yours and You gave them to Me, and they have kept Your word. (John 17:6, *bold highlights added*)

> I am no longer in the world; and yet they themselves are in the world, and I come to You. Holy Father, keep them in Your **name**, the **name** which You have given Me, that they may be one even as we are. While I was with them, I was keeping them in Your **name** which You have given Me; and I guarded them and not one of them perished but the son of perdition, so that the Scripture would be fulfilled. (John 17:11–12, *bold highlights added*)

> O righteous Father, although the world has not known You, yet I have known You; and these have known that You sent Me; and I have made Your **name** known to them, and will make it known, so that the love with which You loved Me may be in them, and I in them. (John 17:25–26, *bold highlights added*)

What name of the Father was the Messiah referring? I doubt if it were *Adonai* or *Kurios*. He was referring to the name that the Judeans had stopped speaking. He was returning the name, YHWH, back to them. He was sent to bring YHWH back into focus for the Israelites who would, later, introduce their Elohim to the Gentiles.

This name, YHWH, is the very name the Messiah shared with his disciples and even spoke raising the ire of the high priests on the night of his arrest. He actually speaks aloud the name YHWH when quoting Psalm 110:1. Our Bibles record him saying, "...hereafter you will see the son of man sitting at the right hand of power..." Keep in mind, the word "power" is one of the many terms the Israelites used instead of saying YHWH. Did the Messiah really use this substitute word or did he say the name? The answer lies in the response of the high priest. Immediately upon hearing the Messiah say the name aloud, the high priest declares that he has committed blasphemy; tearing his own clothes, he says the Messiah's action demands death (Matthew 26:64–65). Saying Elohim's name was clearly forbidden and a capital offense that carried the penalty of death.

Examination of the Talmud gives better insight on this. The Talmud is a collection of the customs, practices, and laws of the Israelite people along with their rabbinical interpretation. It was written in the second century when it was no longer possible for the priests, Levites, and others to gather at the temple to discuss and share their opinions on such matters. The following excerpt from the Babylonian Talmud, Book 8, Tract Sanhedrin, Chapter VII translated by Michael L. Rodkinson in 1918 discusses how one was found guilty of blasphemy and the appropriate response of the judges.

> MISHNA VI.: A blasphemer is not guilty, unless he mentioned the proper name of God (Jehovah). Said R. Jehoshua b. Karha: Through the entire trial the witnesses are examined pseudonymously--i.e. (the blasphemer said): "Jose shall be beaten by Jose." (Rashi explains that the name Jose was selected because it contains four letters, as does the proper name of the Lord.) When the examination was ended, the culprit was not executed on the testimony under the pseudonym; but all are told to leave the room except the witnesses, and the oldest of them is instructed: "Tell what you heard exactly." And he does so. The judges then arise, and rend their garments, and they are not to be mended. The second witness then says: I heard exactly the same as he told. And so also says the third witness.

As you can see, a person is guilty of blasphemy only if he mentions the proper name of Elohim, the four letter name, YHWH. And, there must be two or three witnesses to verify the offense. This is also consistent with the Scriptures which says that the evidence of two or three witnesses must exist to convict a person of a violation of the Law (Deuteronomy 19:15). Finally, the tearing of clothes is the customary response to a confirmed crime of blasphemy. Certainly, the description outlined in Matthews 26 can lead to the conclusion that the Messiah did, indeed, freely speak the name YHWH.

Impact of the Growth of the Body of Believers

Later, non-Israelites or Gentiles were the recipients of the good news of the Messiah, and they were very receptive to the message. The body of believers that was once an Israelite sect was quickly becoming predominantly Gentile. The prevalence of Gentiles in the Church caused many of the Israelite believers to discontinue ties with this new group of believers. It was the Israelite believers who had the historical relationship with the Most High and an understanding of the Hebrew Scriptures. The Israelites who believed in the Messiah did not forsake their worship of YHWH in favor of the Messiah. Instead, they continued to worship the Most High, observing the commandments, statutes, ordinances in their Torah with new understanding because of the Messiah. For this reason, they were known as a sect of the Judeans.

As the successful missionary efforts grew the number of Gentile believers in the Messiah, the Israelite believers experienced cultural challenges because they were beginning to be seen not so much as a sect of the Hebrews, which they were, but now part of a Gentile religion. Therefore, many Israelites no longer wanted to belong to what was becoming a Gentile group, and they cut their ties with the believers. With them went the greater knowledge and historical understanding of Elohim. So as Gentiles began to dominate the Church, the name of YHWH became less prominent among the believers in the Messiah.

Chapter Nine:
Names Do Matter

THE SCRIPTURES TAKE ON A WHOLE DIFFERENT meaning when you read them acknowledging the name YHWH instead of the substitute titles and terms we've been accustomed to reading. We see that He is who He proclaims Himself to be throughout the Old Testament scriptures, where His character and attributes are clearly revealed to us. We see Him when He created the earth in six days and rested on the seventh day. We see His righteous judgment in the flood. We see His loving nature when He chooses Abraham and his seed to be the instruments through whom all the families of the earth would be blessed. It is YHWH, Himself, who announces His attributes when He shows Himself to Moses.

Moses, who had been having many one-on-one conversations with YHWH, wanted to get a glimpse of Him. Because no one has ever seen the Most High and lived, YHWH said He would permit Moses to see only the His posterior or backside as He passes before Moses on the mountain. Just so Moses would be sure that it was indeed Elohim who was passing before him, YHWH would declare His own name to identify Himself.

And YHWH descended in the cloud, and stood there with him, as he called upon the name of YHWH. Then YHWH passed by in front of him and proclaimed, YHWH, YHWH El, compassionate and gracious, slow to anger, and abounding in lovingkindness and truth, who keeps lovingkindness for thousands, who forgives iniquity, transgression and sin; yet He will by no means leave the guilty unpunished; visiting the iniquity of fathers on the children and on the grandchildren to the third and fourth generations." (Exodus 34:5–7)

Some people who vehemently denied the need to acknowledge the sacred name of the Almighty say that it does not matter what we call Him. They say that almost any of the words that people have declared to be His name will pass muster. The argument I have heard by some is that the Most High is wise enough to know Whom we are talking about, and, of course, He knows our hearts.

Well, let's just think about that. We are talking about Elohim who, Himself, has always placed an emphasis on names. Abram had a very good name and was known for many years by that name. Yet, when Abram entered into the covenant relationship with YHWH, He sought to change not just Abram's name to Abraham but also the name of his wife from Sarai to Sarah. This couple went from being Abram and Sarai to the names they have been known by for many centuries. The new names reflect what YHWH had in store for them. Abraham means "father of many nations," which became reality as he was the patriarch of the Israelites and the less-talked-about Ishmaelites. The name Sarah means "princess" or "noble lady," which is a name befitting one of high stature whose descendents would include royalty.

Consider also the grandson of Abraham, Jacob. He found himself struggling with one of the Most High's messengers throughout the night, the eve before he was reunited with his brother Esau. In the course of that struggle, Jacob held onto the leg of the messenger until he received a blessing. This blessing came in the form of a name change. "...Your name shall no longer be Jacob, but Israel; for you have striven with Elohim and with men and have prevailed" (Genesis 32:28). From that moment, Jacob, which means "supplanter," was known as

Israel, meaning "he who strives with El." This is the name that he and his descendents have since been known.

If YHWH finds it important to change people's names to reflect His view of them, then it is not too hard to conceive that He definitely values names and their significance. Time after time in the Scriptures, the Most High declares His own name as YHWH. This is a name that appears to be His alone. It is a name that reveals something about Him in relationship to His creation. Because the name appears to be endearing to Him, it is a name of great importance (see Appendix C).

More Than Just a Sound

Today, names sometimes have significant meanings, but often they are merely just a distinctive word used to distinguish one person from another. However, in the ancient world that the Hebrew Scriptures or Old Testament was written, a name was more than just a few letters put together to form a sound. A name represented something about the bearer of the name. The names that parents gave their children were meant to define them in some exacting way. The name had value to the person to whom it referred and to other people who spoke and referenced it.

If we go back to the first record of the naming of a human being, as found in the Bible, we see where the first man, Adam, named his wife. In Genesis 3:20, it says that the man called his wife's name Chawah, which means "living" in Hebrew. (After the Scriptures had been translated into Greek, Latin, and then English, the English versions record her name as Eve.) The Scriptures say that the man gave her this name "…because she was the mother of all the living." This name was very fitting for the first woman, the one through whom all mankind had its start, don't you think? If we look at the names of others in the Old Testament, we see that their names, also, were not given at random but were used to carefully define their lives.

The most common Hebrew word for "name" found in the Old Testament is šém. This seems to share the same root as the word wšm, which means "sign" or "token" and has the same root as the word "šmh," which means "be high" as a memorial.[29] This word, šém, generally identifies a person, place, or thing as a marker to distinguish it from some other person, place, or thing. Not all men were named Adam even though that word, adam, itself means "man," "mankind," or "ground." This name, Adam, was appropriate for the first man because he was first of all, a man, the first of his kind. And secondly, he was literally from the ground. To name all men Adam would have been confusing, to say the least, but there would have had to be some other means of distinguishing one man from another. It seemed like nomenclature was the way to do this.

Therefore, in order for it to be the most effective, names had to be carefully chosen so that they would convey the nature, essence, or characteristic of the person named. For example, when Isaac and Rebecca gave birth to their twin sons, they named the first born, Esau, and the second born, Jacob. Esau was so named because he was hairy. Jacob, which means "supplanter," was so named because he appeared to be trying to hold his older brother from being the first out of the womb. As the two sons grew older, Jacob proved to be exactly as his name implied, for he tricked his brother out of his birthright and then later took his blessing (Genesis 25:25–34, 27).

A change in name means a change of character. Folk etymology attempts to set forth the original meaning of names, as popularly understood, and sometimes provides an aetiology or explanation. In a narrative containing a number of aetiological elements, Jacob's name is changed to Israel (Genesis 32:28), after he has wrestled at the ford of the Jabbok. The meaning of the new name, Israel, "He who strives with God" or "God strives," represents a popular etymology. Nevertheless, there is a significant change in the character of the crafty Jacob from this time forward. According to M. Reisel, the bestowing of a new name was meant to influence not only the character of the recipient, but his future. Solomon, for example, is given the name Jedidiah, "Beloved of Yah," by Nathan the prophet (2 Samuel

12:25). This theophorous name correctly interprets the statement "YHWH loved him." (2 Sam 12:24).[30]

A Good Name

It is not uncommon in our society to hear it said that a person has a good name. This speaks something about the person's reputation. The same holds true for companies or businesses. Very often when companies are sold, people or businesses will buy the right to use that company's name. A company's intangible value that reflects its customers' loyalty, employees' expertise, and other non-concrete assets is often associated with its name. That is known as the company's goodwill or reputation. From the Hebrew sense, the concept of a name is very similar to this. When we refer to a person as having either a good name or a bad name, the name itself is neither good nor bad, per se. However, the reputation associated with that name has those values. I think we all start out with a good name. It is when we do something of a negative nature, be it intentional or unintentional, that the name itself becomes tarnished. If you have a common name that is shared with others in the population, then you run the risk that your name, without any effort on your part, may become sullied.

Let's say that your name happens to be Jane Smith. You are not the only Jane Smith in the world. It is a common name. It is reported that a Jane Smith robs a bank and is on the run. When people see your name, they begin to associate your name with the bank robber. You would have to almost jump through hoops to prove that you are not the same person. It just happens to be someone else with the same name.

Another example that most can relate to is the name Judas. The Hebrew name for this Greek rendition is Yehudah or Judah, a name we are most likely familiar. With the propensity to give everything a Greek flavor during the Hellenization period, this Hebrew name was presented as Ἰούδας in the Greek text. However, it has been transliterated as Judas in our English Bibles. This was a common name at one point. If we go back to the Old Testament, Jacob's fourth son by Leah was named

Judah. It was this Judah for whom the tribe of Judah took its name. King David was from this tribe, and, consequently, so was the Messiah. The Messiah also had a brother by this name (Matthew 13:55; Mark 6:3). As a matter of fact, the Messiah had two disciples with that same name, Judas Iscariot and Judas the son of James (Luke 6:16; Acts 1:13).

As was the case, it was Judas Iscariot who betrayed the Messiah. The name Judas, after that, seemed to have lost its popularity in some circles. Few people today name their sons Judas, but they will name their sons after the Messiah's other disciples. A boy or man named Judas today could be a fine person. That name, unfortunately, possesses certain implications that many parents would not choose to burden on their offspring. Almost two thousand years after the bad act of a man named Judas, people still shy away from that name.

Well, no matter what century we are talking about, I believe most people have cared about their names. They care about the image it stirs up and what it says about them. Most people want to be viewed as upstanding and have tried, and still strive, to protect their names. It is important that the name of a person is not maligned, because it is difficult to get one's good name back once it has been destroyed.

Chapter Ten:
Protecting *the* Name

Now the sons of Israel journeyed from Rameses to Succoth, about six hundred thousand men on foot, aside from children. A mixed multitude also went up with them, along with flocks and herds, a very large number of livestock. (Exodus 12:37–38)

W HEN ISRAEL WENT TO EGYPT DURING THE days of the famine, the Scriptures says that there were seventy of them in all that came from the land of Canaan. Some four hundred years later, the descendents of Israel had grown to a great number of people. After all, it was because of this growing population that the Egyptian Pharaoh became concerned and enslaved the Israelites. At the time of their Exodus from Egypt, the male Israelite population numbered about six hundred thousand men. It is estimated that there were over two million Israelites including the women and children.

The last plague that YHWH struck on the Egyptians was the death of the first born. Still reeling from the death of his oldest child, a son, and the cries of mourning throughout the land, Pharaoh told Moses to take the Israelites and go. So Israel left. In addition to these two million Israelites, there were included among them other people—some Egyptians and non-Egyptians who had been living in Egypt. These non-Israelites were known as the mixed multitude.

As we know, YHWH had sent Moses to Egypt to deliver the Israelites from the Egyptians and take them to the land of Canaan. The method YHWH had employed to get Israel out of the land of Egypt was pretty dramatic. This was done so that the Egyptians would know that YHWH was passing judgment on them (Exodus 7:3–5, 17; 8:19, 22). Not only did Pharaoh and the Egyptians come to appreciate the power of YHWH through the plagues, but also the Israelites came to know YHWH, their Elohim who acted on their behalf.

The Israelites were coming into a new understanding of YHWH. He was obviously not a power that you could take for granted or minimize. They were learning how to worship Him and be His special people while on their journey to the land of Canaan. That is why, while on the journey, the Israelites were caught off guard when one in their company spoke against the name of YHWH. This particular incident took place after they had over a year to know Him and His expectations of them. It occurred shortly after the tabernacle had been constructed and dedicated (Leviticus 24).

The problem began when two young men, an Israelite man and a mixed birth Egyptian-Israelite man, became engaged in a physical altercation that resulted in some careless words being said. The mixed-birth man blasphemed the name of YHWH, which resulted in everything in the camp coming to a halt. The Israelite people had come to revere YHWH's name. For they knew that dishonoring His name was serious. Moses was sought to find out how this offense should be handled, and he inquired of YHWH. Blaspheming the name of the Most High brought the penalty of death (Leviticus 24:10–16). So, they stoned the man who blasphemed and then resumed their lives.

Blaspheming the Name

It is important to note that after this occurred, the people did not shy away from using the Almighty's name. They dealt with the offender, but they continued to speak YHWH's name. It was not until about seven hundred years later that they actually stopped saying His name.

The man who committed the offense of blasphemy reviled the name of YHWH by signaling it out, possibly, to defame it, which is actually what it means to blaspheme. The people who actually heard the blasphemy had come to a place where they knew that the name YHWH deserved the highest level of respect. Hence, the name should not be treated as if it were common as obviously was done. That is the reason the Israelites responded the way they did.

There are far too many times in the Old Testament where we see that Elohim's name was freely used, even with the penalty of death hanging over the head of anyone who might blaspheme the name. The people were not so afraid to say the name for fear of disrespecting Elohim that they stopped calling out to Him by name. Rather, they were learning to further respect and reverence YHWH. His name was the way to identify and refer to Him. To refrain from using His name would have been true disrespect, especially when Elohim was so freely proclaiming His name to them. Furthermore, consider that even after this act of blasphemy, it is recorded that YHWH actually declared His name at least 20 more times[31] before the Israelites actually entered the Promised Land. The point is that the Most High continued to identify Himself by His name, YHWH. He did this so that the Israelites would know and reverence Him and identify Him by all His works and ways. YHWH obviously did not want to be a nameless power that people referred to in generalities so as to be confused with other elohim who were powerless compared to Him. He wanted to be known for who He is and to be known by name. He called Himself YHWH. The Scriptures bear this over six thousand times.

By: Iris A. Foreman

The Problem of Being Overprotective

The Scriptures also bear the fact that His name is sacred and should be handled with the utmost respect. Many people—from the time of the Judeans' return from Babylon even until today—have appointed themselves as guardians of the name. They act as protectors of this great name. These people know the name, but they choose not to share or speak it with others. Their restraint is not so much because they feel that they themselves may blaspheme the name, but it is because they fear what others may do. These sacred name protectors suppose that making the name a part of common knowledge presents too many risks.

Putting YHWH's name on a shelf and forgetting about it certainly is not giving the name the respect it deserves. It does not honor the Most High, either, despite what some may think. YHWH states His own displeasure with those who cause others to forget His name (Jeremiah 23:25ff). Yet, history tells us that this is exactly what has happened. After the Babylonian exile, false teaching occurred that resulted in a restriction of the use of YHWH's name. As time progressed, fewer and fewer people were permitted to say the name, and as a result, fewer people even knew it. People feared profaning the name and stopped speaking it. YHWH never did prohibit them from saying it. Their desire to get serious about serving YHWH spilled into an overzealousness that led to some inappropriate decisions and false doctrines.

This decision had disastrous results. Over time, because the name was not spoken or read aloud, the people eventually forgot the name. Unfortunately, people who have truly wanted to have a relationship with Elohim have been shortchanged because they have not known Him by name.

Today's Arguments

Today, we do not need to protect YHWH's name to such a degree that we do not use it at all. The best way to protect it is by honoring it. We protect it by giving it its rightful place. There is no greater way to protect His name than by reverencing it as we reverence the One to whom it belongs. It is not necessary for us to refrain from saying the name just to protect others from stumbling over it. We must use it. We cannot properly call out to YHWH without calling His true name. The Scriptures says that when the day of YHWH comes, those that call upon His name will be delivered and heard by Him (Joel 2:32; Zechariah 13:9).[32]

Too often I have heard—and have even been guilty of saying it myself—that we should not use the Almighty's name because others may use it in vain. We think about the way people curse by saying "goddamn" or exclaim "Jesus Christ" as a form of profanity, so we assume, rightfully so, they will do even worse if His name was known. Nothing seems sacred in our society anymore. And, it is almost a challenge to some wicked people to desecrate anything others seem to hold as sacred. So, it is not without reason that one would want to protect such a precious name as YHWH. However, this really is not a valid reason not to use the name. If people choose to sin in this manner, then we who refer to the Most High by His name are not responsible for their sins. We must make certain that we, ourselves, do not misuse the name.

Maybe the decision of not addressing Him by name may be based on choosing not to be offensive to others who do not believe in Him. As the saying goes, "You can win more flies with honey than you can with vinegar." This may, somehow, apply in this case. Our non-committal, verbal claim to a particular el has made it so that we do not actually take a stand for YHWH. By not using His name, we leave it to others to draw their own conclusions about to whom we may be referring when we say terms such as *God* and *Lord*. This brings to mind the secular Twelve-Step programs, such as Alcoholics Anonymous, which use the term "Higher Power" instead of "god." Almost everyone believes in some form of a higher power; some refer to theirs in general terms such as "god" while others may have specific personal names. Rather than offend other Twelve-Step meeting participants, the non-specific and very general term "Higher Power" is used. By choosing not to say the name YHWH, we are essentially doing the same thing that they do in these programs. We are not identifying Him. We are not owning Him as ours. We are denying Him.

Believe it or not, many people already say His name without consciously being aware of this. If you say "Halleluyah" (sometimes spelled "Hallelujah"), then you are actually saying a shortened, poetic version of the name YHWH. This word, halleluyah, is composed of two Hebrew words. The first part of the word is the verb, *halal*, which means "to praise." The second part of the word is none other than *Yah*, the name of the Most High. "HalleluYah" is Hebrew for "Praise Yah!"

Protecting His name from other people is not our responsibility. YHWH is more than capable of protecting His name and dealing with anyone who intentionally abuses it. If we are to be true worshipers of the Elohim of Abraham, Isaac, and Jacob, then we need to really worship Him in spirit and in truth. Worship Him openly and freely. Declare His name. Call upon His holy and righteous name.

Chapter Eleven:
Let's Get Acquainted
With YHWH

THERE IS SO MUCH IN THE Old Testament Scriptures that will give us a better insight into YHWH, the Mighty One of the Israelites. However, a lot is missed by most Bible readers because the Most High is presented in general terms such as "God" and not as the specific, definitive entity that He really is. Christians have been taught and many believe in this nebulous god. If we do not name Him, then He really is no more than a non-descript entity. He is not the fullness of YHWH, who is so awesomely portrayed in the ancient text that we call the Bible.

For those of us who want to truly know the Mighty One of Israel, a greater appreciation and awareness of Him comes when we start to say and use His true, personal name, YHWH. So how should you pronounce YHWH? My personal preference is Yahwah, but others pronounce it differently as discussed earlier in this book. It is better to attempt to say His name than to completely ignore it. After all, His name is important to Him, so it also should be important to His servants, those of us who say we worship Him.

To really get to know YHWH, we should begin to refer to Him by name. There is something special that comes to the relationship you have with Him when this is done. It is called intimacy.

To build upon that intimacy, I encourage you to begin to read the Scriptures again. Start in Genesis and work your way through to Revelation. This time, however, undo the works of the translators who have put the words "the LORD" where YHWH should be. Instead of reading "the LORD," read "YHWH" just as it should have always been. You will see Him anew, in a more real and personal way.

It is time. Let's get acquainted with YHWH. Let's call Him by His name, YHWH.

Appendix A:
Editor Notes and
Translators Notes

New Living Translation

Life Application Study Bible, Tyndale House Publishers, Wheaton, IL, 2004

In the Introduction to the New Living Translation found in the front of the Bible, it reads...

The Rendering of Divine Names

All appearances of *'el, 'elohim,* or *'eloah* have been translated "God," except where the context demands the translation "god(s)." We have generally rendered the tetragrammaton (*YHWH*) consistently as "YHWH," utilizing a form with small capitals that is common among English translations. This will distinguish it from the name *'adonai,* which we render "Lord." When *'adonai* and *YHWH* appear together, we have rendered it "Sovereign LORD." This also distinguish *'adonai YHWH* from cases where *YHWH* appears with *'elohim,* which is rendered "LORD God." When *YH* (the short form of *YHWH* appear with the term *tseba'oth*, we have rendered it "LORD of Heaven's Armies" to translate the meaning of the name. In a few cases, we have utilized the transliteration, *YHWH*, when the personal character of the name is being invoked in contrast to any other divine name or the name of some other god (For example, see Exod 3:15, 6:2-3)"

The Good News Translation

My Book. — God, Zondervan,Grand Rapid,1992

In the Preface of the Bible, it gives the following explanation for the translation of the Most High's name.

> Following an ancient tradition, begun by the first translation of the Hebrew Scriptures into Greek (the Septuagint) and followed by the vast majority of English translations, the distinctive Hebrew Name for God (usually transliterated *Jehovah* or *YHWH*) is in this translation represented by "LORD." When *Adonai*, normally translated "Lord," is followed by *YHWH*, the combination is rendered by the phrase "Sovereign LORD."

New American Standard Bible

Life Application Study Bible, Zondervan, Grand Rapids, 2000

In the Section entitled *Principles of Translation*, page xi, it states....

> THE PROPER NAME OF GOD IN THE OLD
> TESTAMENT: In the Scriptures, the name of God
> is most significant, and understandably so. It is
> inconceivable to think of spiritual matters without a
> proper designation for the Supreme Deity. Thus the
> most common name for the Deity is God, a translation
> of the original *Elohim*. One of the titles of God is Lord,
> a translation of *Adonai*. There is yet another name which
> is particularly assigned to God as His special or proper
> name, that is, the four letters YHWH (Exodus 3:14 and
> Isaiah 42:8). This name has not been pronounced by
> the Jews because of reverence for the great sacredness
> of the divine name. Therefore, it has been consistently
> LORD. The only exception to this translation of
> YHWH is when it occurs in immediate proximity to
> the word Lord, that is, *Adonai*. In that case it is regularly
> translated GOD in order to avoid confusion.
>
> It is known that for many years YHWH has been
> transliterated as YHWH; however no complete
> certainty attaches to this pronunciation.

New King James Version

Experiencing God Study Bible, Broadman & Holman Publishers, Nashville, 1994

In the Preface to the NKJV on page xxiii, the following brief statement
is made.

> The covenant name of God was usually translated
> from the Hebrew as "LORD" or "GOD" (usually capital

letters as shown) in the King James Old Testament. This tradition is maintained. In the present edition the name is so capitalized whenever the covenant name is quoted in the New Testament from a passage in the Old Testament.

New International Version

International Inductive Study Bible, Harvest House Publisher, Eugene, OR, 1995

It states in the Preface, page iv:

> In regard to the divine name *YHWH*, commonly referred to as the *Tetragrammaton*, the translators adopted the device used in most English versions of rendering that name as "LORD" in capital letters to distinguish it from *Adonai*, another Hebrew word rendered "Lord," for which small letters are used. Wherever the two names stand together in the Old Testament as a compound name of God, they are rendered "Sovereign LORD."

New Revised Standard Bible

The New Oxford Annotated Bible, Oxford University Press, 2007

The following is included in the Reader Section on page xx:

Careful readers will notice that here and there in the Old

Testament the word LORD (or in certain cases GOD) is printed in capital letters. This represents the traditional manner in English versions of rendering the Divine Name, the "Tetragrammaton" (see the translation note on Exodus 3.14,15), following the precedent of the Ancient Greek and Latin translators and the long established practice in the reading of the Hebrew Scriptures in the synagogue. While it is almost if not quite certain that the Name was originally pronounced "Yahweh," this pronunciation was not indicated when the Masoretes added vowel sounds to the consonantal Hebrew text. To the four consonants YHWH of the Name, which had come to be regarded as too sacred to be pronounced, they attached vowel signs indicating that in its place should be read the Hebrew word *Adonai* meaning "Lord" (or *Elohim* meaning "God"). Ancient Greek translators employed the word *Kyrios* ("Lord") for the Name. The Vulgate likewise used the Latin word *Dominus* ("Lord"). The form "Jehovah" is of the late medieval origin; it is a combination of the consonants of the Divine Name and the vowels attached to it by the Masoretes but belonging to an entirely different word. Although the American Standard Version (1901) had used "Jehovah" to render the Tetragrammaton (the sound of Y being represented by J and the sound of W by V, as in Latin), for two reasons the Committees that produced the RSV and the NRSV returned to the more familiar usage of the King James Version. (1) The word "Jehovah" does not accurately represent any form of the Name ever used in Hebrew. (2) The use of any proper name for the one and only God, as thought there were other gods from whom the true God had to be distinguished, began to be discontinued in Judaism before the Christian era and is inappropriate for the universal faith of the Christian Church.

By: Iris A. Foreman

English Standard Version

The Holy Bible, Crossway- a ministry of Good News Publishing in Wheaton, IL, 2001

It states the following on page ix in the Preface:

> In the translation of the biblical terms referring
> to God, the ESV takes care to convey the specific
> nuances of meaning of the original Hebrew and Greek
> terms. First, concerning terms that refer to God in
> the Old Testament: God, the maker of heaven and
> earth, introduced himself to the people of Israel with
> the special, personal name, whose consonants are
> YHWH (see Exodus 3:14–15). Scholars call this the
> "Tetragrammaton," a Greek term referring to the
> four Hebrew letters YHWH. The exact pronunciation
> of YHWH is uncertain, because the Jewish people
> considered the personal name of God to be so holy that
> it should never be spoken aloud. Instead of reading the
> word YHWH, they would normally read the Hebrew
> word *adonai* ("Lord"), and the ancient translations
> into Greek, Syriac, and Aramaic also followed suit.
> When the vowels of the word *adonai* are placed with
> the consonants of YHWH, this results in the familiar
> word *Jehovah* that was used in some earlier English Bible
> translations. As is common among English translations
> today, the ESV usually renders the personal name of
> God (YHWH) with the word LORD (printed in small
> capitals). An exception to this is when the Hebrew word
> *adonai* appears together with YHWH, in which case
> the two words are rendered together as "the Lord [in
> lower case] GOD [in small capitals]." In contrast to the
> personal name of God (YHWH), the more general
> name for God in Old Testament Hebrew is *'elohim* and
> its related forms of *'el* or *'eloah*, all of which are normally
> translated "God" (in lower case letters). The use of
> these different ways to translate the Hebrew words

for God is especially beneficial to the English reader, enabling the reader to see and understand the different ways that the *personal* name and the *general* name for God are both used to refer to the *One True God* of the Old Testament.

New American Standard Bible

Life Application Study Bible, Zondervan in Grand Rapids, Michigan, 2000

It contains the following text in the Principles of Translation section on page xi:

> In the Scriptures, the name of God is most significant, and understandably so. It is inconceivable to think of spiritual matters without a proper designation for the Supreme Deity. Thus the most common name for the Deity is God, a translation of the original *Elohim*. One of the titles for God is Lord, a translation of *Adonai*. There is yet another name which is particularly assigned to God as His special or proper name, that is, the four letters YHWH (Exodus 3:14 and Isaiah 42:8). This name has not been pronounced by the Jews because of reverence for the great sacredness of the divine name. Therefore, it has been consistently translated LORD. The only exception to this translation of YHWH is when it occurs in immediate proximity to the word Lord, that is, *Adonai*. In that case it is regularly translated GOD in order to avoid confusion.

> It is known that for many years YHWH has been transliterated as Yahweh; however no complete certainty attaches to this pronunciation.

Appendix B:
The Name of YHWH in Scripture

The name YHWH appears in the Bible thousands of times. Without question His name exists. The arguments that name of Elohim is not important can be dispelled when faced with the scriptures. Biblical texts tell us that His name is great, awesome, holy, everlasting, and much more. We also find verses in the Scriptures which identify His name as YHWH. The verses referenced herein are listed to assist the reader in her or his study of this particular topic.

Please be aware that every instance where the terms *the LORD* and *God* appear in the quoted biblical text has been changed. The words *YHWH* and *El* or *Elohim* have been re-inserted to reflect the original language and intent.

Call or Called Upon the Name

Genesis 4:26 And to Seth, to him also a son was born; and he called his name Enosh. Then *men* began to call upon the name of YHWH.

Genesis 12:8 Then he proceeded from there to the mountain on the east of Bethel, and pitched his tent, with Bethel on the west and Ai on the east; and there he built an altar to YHWH and called upon the name of YHWH.

Genesis 13:4 to the place of the altar, which he had made there formerly; and there Abram called on the name of YHWH.

Genesis 21:33 And *Abraham* planted a tamarisk tree at Beersheba, and there he called on the name of YHWH, the Everlasting El.

Genesis 26:25 So he built an altar there, and called upon the name of YHWH, and pitched his tent there; and there Isaac's servants dug a well.

Isaiah 12:4 And in that day you will say, "Give thanks to YHWH, call on His name. Make known His deeds among the peoples; Make *them* remember that His name is exalted."

Holy Name

YHWH refers to His own name as being holy

Leviticus 20:3 'I will also set My face against that man and will cut him off from among his people, because he has given some of his offspring to Molech, so as to defile My sanctuary and to profane My holy name.

Leviticus 22:2 "Tell Aaron and his sons to be careful with the holy *gifts* of the sons of Israel, which they dedicate to Me, so as not to profane My holy name; I am YHWH.

Leviticus 22:32 "And you shall not profane My holy name, but I will be sanctified among the sons of Israel: I am YHWH who sanctifies you,

Ezekiel 20:39 "As for you, O house of Israel," thus says Adonai YHWH, "Go, serve everyone his idols; but later, you will surely listen to Me, and My holy name you will profane no longer with your gifts and with your idols.

Additional verses:

Ezekiel 36:20-21; 39:7, 25; 43:7-8; Amos 2:7

His name is referred to by others as holy

1 Chronicles 16:10 Glory in His holy name; Let the heart of those who seek YHWH be glad.

1 Chronicles 16:35 Then say, "Save us, O Elohim of our salvation, And gather us and deliver us from the nations, To give thanks to Your holy name, And glory in Your praise."

1 Chronicles 29:16 "YHWH our Elohim, all this abundance that we have provided to build You a house for Your holy name, it is from Your hand, and all is Yours.

Psalm 33:21 For our heart rejoices in Him, Because we trust in His holy name.

Additional verses:

Psalm 103:1; 105:3; 106:47; 145:21; Isaiah 57:15

Awesome (Fearful) Name

Deuteronomy 28:58 "If you are not careful to observe all the words of this law which are written in this book, to fear this honored and awesome name, YHWH your Elohim,

Great Name

Joshua 7:9 "For the Canaanites and all the inhabitants of the land will hear of it, and they will surround us and cut off our name from the earth. And what wilt Thou do for Thy great name?"

1 Kings 8:42 (for they will hear of Your great name and Your mighty hand, and of Your outstretched arm); when he comes and prays toward this house,

Jeremiah 44:26 "Nevertheless hear the word of YHWH, all Judah who are living in the land of Egypt, 'Behold, I have sworn by My great name,' says YHWH, 'never shall My name be invoked again by the mouth of any man of Judah in all the land of Egypt, saying, "As Adonai YHWH lives."

Ezekiel 36:23 "And I will vindicate the holiness of My great name which has been profaned among the nations, which you have profaned in their midst. Then the nations will know that I am YHWH," declares Adonai YHWH, "when I prove Myself holy among you in their sight.

Glorious Name

1 Chronicles 29:13 "Now therefore, our Elohim, we thank You, and praise Your glorious name.

Nehemiah 9:5 Then the Levites, Jeshua, Kadmiel, Bani, Hashabneiah, Sherebiah, Hodiah, Shebaniah, *and* Pethahiah, said, "Arise, bless YHWH your Elohim forever and ever! O may Your glorious name be blessed And exalted above all blessing and praise!

Psalm 72:19 And blessed be His glorious name forever; And may the whole earth be filled with His glory. Amen, and Amen.

Isaiah 63:14 As the cattle which go down into the valley, The Spirit of YHWH gave them rest. So You led Your people, To make for Yourself a glorious name.

Great and Awesome (Terrible) Name

Psalm 99:3 Let them praise Your great and awesome name; Holy is He.

Everlasting Name

Isaiah 63:12 Who caused His glorious arm to go at the right hand of Moses, Who divided the waters before them to make for Himself an everlasting name,

Exodus 3:15 And Elohim, furthermore, said to Moses,

"Thus you shall say to the sons of Israel, 'YHWH, the Elohim of your fathers, the Elohim of Abraham, the Elohim of Isaac, and the Elohim of Jacob, has sent me to you.' This is My name forever, and this is My memorial-name to all generations.

Name of Elohim

Ezra 5:1 When the prophets, Haggai the prophet and Zechariah the son of Iddo, prophesied to the Jews who were in Judah and Jerusalem, in the name of the El of Israel, who was over them,

Psalm 20:1 *For the choir director. A Psalm of David* May YHWH answer you in the day of trouble! May the name of the God of Jacob set you *securely* on high!

Psalm 20:5 We will sing for joy over your victory, And in the name of our God we will set up our banners. May YHWH fulfill all your petitions.

Psalm 44:20 If we had forgotten the name of our God, Or extended our hands to a strange god;

Additional verses:

Psalm 69:30; Proverbs 30:9; Daniel 2:20

My Name

Exodus 6:3 and I appeared to Abraham, Isaac, and

Jacob, as God Almighty, but *by* My name, YHWH, I did not make Myself known to them.

Exodus 9:16 "But, indeed, for this cause I have allowed you to remain, in order to show you My power, and in order to proclaim My name through all the earth.

Exodus 20:24 'You shall make an altar of earth for Me, and you shall sacrifice on it your burnt offerings and your peace offerings, your sheep and your oxen; in every place where I cause My name to be remembered, I will come to you and bless you.

Additional verses:

Exodus 23:21; Leviticus 19:12; 20:3; Numbers 6:27; Deuteronomy 18:19-20; 2 Samuel 7:13; 1 Kings 5:5; 8:16, 18, 20, 29; 1 Kings 9:3, 7; 1 Kings 11:36; 2 Kings 21:4, 7; 1 Chronicles 22:10; 28:3; 2 Chronicles 6:5-6, 8-9;7:14, 16, 20; 33:4, 7; Nehemiah 1:9; Psalm 89:24; 91:14; Isaiah 29:23; 41:25; 42:8; 43:7; 52:5-6; 65:1; Jeremiah 7:10-12, 14, 30; 12:16; 14:14-15; 16:21; 23:25, 27; 25:29; 27:15; 29:9, 21, 23; 32:34; 34:15-16; 44:26; Amos 9:12; Zechariah 5:4; 13:9; Malachi 1:6, 11, 14; 2:2, 5; 4:2

YHWH Is His Name

Exodus 15:3 "YHWH is a warrior; YHWH is His name.

Jeremiah 48:15 "Moab has been destroyed, and men have gone up to his cities; His choicest young men have also gone down to the slaughter," Declares the King, whose name is YHWH of hosts.

Jeremiah 51:57 "I will make her princes and her wise men drunk, Her governors, her prefects, and her mighty men, That they may sleep a perpetual sleep and not wake up," Declares the King, whose name is YHWH of hosts.

Name of the Father

Matthew 28:19 "Go therefore and make disciples of all the nations, baptizing them in the name of the Father and the Son and the Holy Spirit,

John 5:43 "I have come in My Father's name, and you do not receive Me; if another shall come in his own name, you will receive him.

John 10:25 Jesus answered them, "I told you, and you do not believe; the works that I do in My Father's name, these bear witness of Me.

Name of YHWH

Exodus 20:7 "You shall not take the name of YHWH your God in vain, for YHWH will not leave him unpunished who takes His name in vain.

Exodus 33:19 And He said, "I Myself will make all My goodness pass before you, and will proclaim the name of YHWH before you; and I will be gracious to whom I will be gracious, and will show compassion on whom I will show compassion."

Exodus 34:5 YHWH descended in the cloud and stood there with him as he called upon the name of YHWH.

Leviticus 24:16 'Moreover, the one who blasphemes the name of YHWH shall surely be put to death; all the congregation shall certainly stone him. The alien as well as the native, when he blasphemes the Name, shall be put to death.

Deuteronomy 5:11 'You shall not take the name of YHWH your God in vain, for YHWH will not leave him unpunished who takes His name in vain.

Additional verses:

Deuteronomy 18:5, 7, 22; 21:5; 28:10; 32:3; Joshua 9:9; 1 Samuel 17:45; 20:42; 1 Kings 10:1; 18:24, 32; 22:16; 2 Kings 2:24; 5:11; 1 Chronicles 16:2; 22:7, 19; 2 Chronicles 2:1, 4; 6:7, 6:10; 18:15; 33:18; Job 1:21; Psalm 7:17; 20:7; 102:15, 21; 113:1-3; 116:4, 13, 17; 118:10-12, 26; 122:4; 124:8; 135:1; 148:5, 13; Proverbs 18:10; Isaiah 18:7; 24:15; 30:27; 48:1; 50:10; 56:6; 59:19; 60:9; Jeremiah 3:17; 11:21; 26:9, 16, 20; 44:16; Joel 2:26, 32; Amos 6:10; Micah 4:5; 5:4; Zephaniah 3:9, 12; 13:3; Matthew 21:9; Mark 11:9; Luke 13:35; 19:38; John 12:13; Acts 2:21

Name of Your or Their Elohim

Leviticus 18:21 You shall not give any of your offspring to offer them to Molech, nor shall you profane the name of your God; I am YHWH.

Leviticus 19:12 You shall not swear falsely by My name, so as to profane the name of your God; I am YHWH.

Leviticus 21:6 'They shall be holy to their God and not profane the name of their God, for they present the offerings by fire to YHWH, the food of their God; so they shall be holy.

Thy or Your Name

2 Samuel 22:50 "Therefore I will give thanks to Thee, O YHWH, among the nations, And I will sing praises to Thy name.

1 Kings 8:33 "When Your people Israel are defeated before an enemy, because they have sinned against You, if they turn to You again and confess Your name and pray and make supplication to You in this house,

1 Kings 8:35 "When the heavens are shut up and there is no rain, because they have sinned against You, and they pray toward this place and confess Your name and turn from their sin when You afflict them,

1 Kings 8:43 hear in heaven Your dwelling place, and do according to all for which the foreigner calls to You, in order that all the peoples of the earth may know Your name, to fear You, as do Your people Israel, and that they may know that this house which I have built is called by Your name.

1 Kings 8:44 "When Your people go out to battle against their enemy, by whatever way You shall send them, and they pray to YHWH toward the city which You have chosen and the house which I have built for Your name,

1 Kings 8:48 if they return to You with all their heart and with all their soul in the land of their enemies who

have taken them captive, and pray to You toward their land which You have given to their fathers, the city which You have chosen, and the house which I have built for Your name;

Additional verses:

1 Kings 18:31; 1 Chronicles 17:24; 2 Chronicles 6:20, 24, 26, 33-34, 38; 14:11; 20:8-9; Nehemiah 1:11; Psalm 5:11; 8:1, 9; 9:2, 10; 18:49; 22:22; 44:5, 8; 45:17; 48:10; 52:9; 54:1, 6; 61:5, 8; 63:4; 66:4; 74:7, 10, 18, 21; 75:1; 79:6, 9; 80:18; 83:16; 86:9, 11-12; 89:16; 92:1; 115:1; 119:55, 132; 135:13; 138:2; 139:20; 140:13; 142:7; 145:1-2; 148:13; Isaiah 25:1; 26:8, 13; 63:16, 19; 64:2, 7; Jeremiah 10:6, 25; 14:9; 15:16;

Lamentations 3:55; Daniel 9:18-19; Malachi 1:6; Matthew 6:9; Luke 11:2; John 12:28; 17:6, 11-12, 26

His Name

Deuteronomy 10:8 At that time YHWH set apart the tribe of Levi to carry the ark of the covenant of YHWH, to stand before YHWH to serve Him and to bless in His name until this day.

Deuteronomy 6:13 "You shall fear *only* YHWH your God; and you shall worship Him, and swear by His name.

Deuteronomy 10:20 "You shall fear YHWH your God; you shall serve Him and cling to Him, and you shall swear by His name.

Deuteronomy 12:5 "But you shall seek *YHWH* at

the place which YHWH your God shall choose from all your tribes, to establish His name there for His dwelling, and there you shall come.

Additional verses:

Deuteronomy 12:11, 21; 16:2, 6, 11; 26:2; 1 Kings 14:21; 1 Chronicles 16:8, 29; 1 Chronicles 23:13; 2 Chronicles 12:13; Ezra 6:12; Psalm 29:2; 34:3; 66:2; 68:4; 69:36; 72:17; 76:1; 96:2, 8; 99:6; 100:4; 105:1; 111:9; 135:3; 149:3; Isaiah 12:4; 47:4; 48:2; Jeremiah 10:16; 20:9; 23:6; 31:35; 32:18; 33:2; 50:34; 51:19; Amos 4:13; 5:8, 27; 9:6; Zechariah 10:12; 14:9; Malachi 3:16

Appendix C:
"I Am YHWH" Scriptures

The Scriptures record over 160 times when the Almighty proclaims His name as YHWH. These scriptures are predominately found in the first five books of the Bible and, occasionally, in the books of the prophets. The fact that the Scripture records this declaration so often supports the importance we can assume the Almighty has for His own name.

Please be aware that every instance where the terms *the LORD* and *God* appear in the quoted biblical text has been changed. The words *YHWH* and *El* or *Elohim* have been re-inserted to reflect the original language and intent.

> Genesis 15:7 And He said to him, "I am YHWH who brought you out of Ur of the Chaldeans, to give you this land to possess it."

> Genesis 28:13 And behold, YHWH stood above it and said, "I am YHWH, the God of your father Abraham and the God of Isaac; the land on which you lie, I will give it to you and to your descendants.

> Exodus 6:2 God spoke further to Moses and said to him, "I am YHWH;

> Exodus 6:6 "Say, therefore, to the sons of Israel, 'I am YHWH, and I will bring you out from under the burdens of the Egyptians, and I will deliver you

from their bondage. I will also redeem you with an outstretched arm and with great judgments.

Exodus 6:7 'Then I will take you for My people, and I will be your God; and you shall know that I am YHWH your God, who brought you out from under the burdens of the Egyptians.

Exodus 6:8 'And I will bring you to the land which I swore to give to Abraham, Isaac, and Jacob, and I will give it to you *for* a possession; I am YHWH.'"

Additional verses in Exodus:

Exodus 6:29; 7:5, 17; 10:2; 12:12; 14:4, 18; 16:12; 20:2; 29:46; 31:13

Leviticus 11:44 'For I am YHWH your God. Consecrate yourselves therefore, and be holy; for I am holy. And you shall not make yourselves unclean with any of the swarming things that swarm on the earth.

Leviticus 11:45 'For I am YHWH, who brought you up from the land of Egypt, to be your God; thus you shall be holy for I am holy.'"

Leviticus 18:2 "Speak to the sons of Israel and say to them, 'I am YHWH your God.

Leviticus 18:4 'You are to perform My judgments and keep My statutes, to live in accord with them; I am YHWH your God.

Additional verses in Leviticus:

Leviticus 18:5-6, 21, 30; 19:3-4, 10, 12, 14, 16, 18, 25, 28, 30-32, 34, 36-37; 20:7-8, 24; 21:12, 15, 23; 22:2-3, 8-9, 16, 30-33; 23:22, 43; 24:22; 25:17, 38, 55; 26:1-2, 13, 44-45

Numbers 3:13 "For all the first-born are Mine; on the day that I struck down all the first-born in the land of Egypt, I sanctified to Myself all the first-born in Israel, from man to beast. They shall be Mine; I am YHWH."

Numbers 3:41 "And you shall take the Levites for Me, I am YHWH, instead of all the first-born among the sons of Israel, and the cattle of the Levites instead of all the first-born among the cattle of the sons of Israel."

Numbers 3:45 "Take the Levites instead of all the first-born among the sons of Israel and the cattle of the Levites. And the Levites shall be Mine; I am YHWH.

Numbers 10:10 "Also in the day of your gladness and in your appointed feasts, and on the first *days* of your months, you shall blow the trumpets over your burnt offerings, and over the sacrifices of your peace offerings; and they shall be as a reminder of you before your God. I am YHWH your God."

Numbers 15:41 "I am YHWH your God who brought you out from the land of Egypt to be your God; I am YHWH your God."

Deuteronomy 5:6 I am YHWH your God, who brought you out of the land of Egypt, out of the house of slavery.

Deuteronomy 29:6 You have not eaten bread, nor have you drunk wine or strong drink, in order that you might know that I am YHWH your God.

Judges 6:10 and I said to you, "I am YHWH your God; you shall not fear the gods of the Amorites in whose land you live. But you have not obeyed Me."'"

1 Kings 20:13 Now behold, a prophet approached Ahab king of Israel and said, "Thus says YHWH, 'Have you seen all this great multitude? Behold, I will deliver them

into your hand today, and you shall know that I am YHWH.'"

1 Kings 20:28 Then a man of God came near and spoke to the king of Israel and said, "Thus says YHWH, 'Because the Arameans have said, "YHWH is a god of *the* mountains, but He is not a god of *the* valleys"; therefore I will give all this great multitude into your hand, and you shall know that I am YHWH.'"

Isaiah 41:13 "For I am YHWH your God, who upholds your right hand, Who says to you, 'Do not fear, I will help you.'

Isaiah 42:6 "I am YHWH, I have called you in righteousness, I will also hold you by the hand and watch over you, And I will appoint you as a covenant to the people, As a light to the nations,

Isaiah 42:8 "I am YHWH, that is My name; I will not give My glory to another, Nor My praise to graven images.

Isaiah 43:3 "For I am YHWH your God, The Holy One of Israel, your Savior; I have given Egypt as your ransom, Cush and Seba in your place.

Isaiah 43:11 "I, even I, am YHWH; And there is no savior besides Me.

Additional verses in Isaiah:

Isaiah 43:15; 45:5-7, 18; 48:17; 49:23; 51:15

Jeremiah 9:24 but let him who boasts boast of this, that he understands and knows Me, that I am YHWH who exercises lovingkindness, justice, and righteousness on earth; for I delight in these things," declares YHWH.

Jeremiah 24:7 'And I will give them a heart to know Me, for I am YHWH; and they will be My people, and

I will be their God, for they will return to Me with their whole heart.

Ezekiel 6:7 "And the slain will fall among you, and you will know that I am YHWH.

Ezekiel 6:10 "Then they will know that I am YHWH; I have not said in vain that I would inflict this disaster on them.'"

Additional verses in Ezekiel:

Ezekiel 6:13-14; 7:4, 27; 11:10, 12, 15-16, 20; 13:14, 21, 23; 14:8; 15:7; 16:62; 17:24; 20:5, 7, 12, 19-20, 26, 38, 42, 44; 22:16; 23:49; 24:24, 24:27; 25:5, 7, 11, 17; 26:6; 28:22-24, 26; 29:6, 9, 16, 21; 30:8, 19, 25-26; 32:15; 33:29; 34:27; 35:4, 9; 35:15; 36:11, 23, 38; 37:6, 13, 28; 38:23; 39:6-39:7, 22, 28

Joel 2:27 "Thus you will know that I am in the midst of Israel, And that I am YHWH your Elohim, And there is no other; And My people will never be put to shame.

Joel 3:17 Then you will know that I am YHWH your Elohim, Dwelling in Zion, My holy mountain. So Jerusalem will be holy, And strangers will pass through it no more.

Zechariah 10:6 I will strengthen the house of Judah, And I will save the house of Joseph, And I will bring them back, Because I have had compassion on them; And they will be as though I had not rejected them, For I am YHWH their Elohim and I will answer them.

Endnotes

1. The fact that Elohim (plural) is used in referencing the Creator is not to infer that there were many gods who were involved in creation, as most Bible readers already well know. But Elohim is used as a singular, albeit in plural form, formal, respectful title that may signify magnitude of greatness.

2. Chad Brand, Charles Draper, and Archie England, eds., Holman Illustrated Bible Dictionary, El, James Newell, (Nashville: Holman Bible Publishers, 2003), 470.

3. There are numerous references to other gods besides YHWH in the Old Testament. For example, "But every nation still made gods of its own and put them in the houses of the high places which the people of Samaria had made, every nation in their cities in which they lived. The men of Babylon made Succoth-benoth, the men of Cuth made Nergal, the men of Hamath made Ashima, and the Avvites made Nibhaz and Tartak; and the Sepharvites burned their children in the fire to Adrammelech and Anammelech the gods of Sepharvaim," (2 Kings 17:29–31). The other nations all had their various gods that they worshiped. Israel was constantly interacting with these people and being exposed to their practices of worship. Sadly, the temptation to worship the gods of the nations, instead of and in addition to YHWH, many times, was too strong for whatever reason.

4. This is a supposition that obviously is not a fact nor can

it be verified. Noah, in all likelihood, did speak the same language that his immediate forefather's spoke. Because many of the people in the pre-flood period lived what we consider long lives (900 years plus), it is not inconceivable to think that their grandsons, great- and great-grandsons lived in close proximity to them and were able to communicate with their grandparents. Biblical accounts point out that Adam lived for 930 years which was 56 years after Noah's father, Lamech, was born. It is possible that Noah's father, his grandfather, Methuselah, or his great-grandfather, Enoch, personally knew Adam, their patriarch. It is also within the realm of reason that they all shared the same language.

5. John Huehnergard, The American Heritage® Dictionary of the English Language, Fourth Edition: *Proto-Semitic Language and Culture*, (Houghton – Mifflin Company, New York, 2000), 2061.

6. John Huehnergard, The American Heritage® Dictionary of the English Language, Fourth Edition: *Proto-Semitic Language and Culture*, (Houghton – Mifflin Company, New York, 2000), 2056-2057.

7. Spiros Zodhiates, The Complete WordStudy New Testament, *Lexical Aids*, (Chattanooga: AMG Publishers, 1991), 920.

8. Ibid.

9. International Standard Bible Encyclopedia, Vol. 2, 505.

10. Zodhiates, 920.

11. http://www.bible-researcher.com/luther02.html. The following is a chapter taken from Philip Schaff's History of the Christian Church (New York: Charles Scribner's Sons, 1910).

12. http://www.bible-researcher.com/tyndale4.html, "English

Versions" by Sir Frederic G. Kenyon in the Dictionary of the Bible edited by James Hastings, and published by Charles Scribner's Sons of New York in 1909.

13. http://www.bible-researcher.com/1911-coverdale.html, "Miles Coverdale", Article from the Encyclopedia Britannica, 11th edition (1911).

14. It's interesting to note the etymology of the word "giddy." "The word *giddy* refers to fairly lightweight experiences or situations, but at one time it had to do with profundities. *Giddy* can be traced back to the same Germanic root **gud–* that has given us the word *God*. The Germanic word **gudigaz* formed on this root meant "possessed by a god." Such possession can be a rather unbalancing experience, and so it is not surprising that the Old English descendant of **gudigaz*, *gidig*, meant "mad, possessed by an evil spirit," or that the Middle English development of *gidig*, *gidi*, meant the same thing, as well as "foolish; mad (used of an animal); dizzy; uncertain, unstable." Our sense "lighthearted, frivolous" represents the ultimate secularization of *giddy*." From The American Heritage® Dictionary of the English Language: Fourth Edition. 2006, 742.

15. Douglas Harper, Online Etymology Dictionary, http://www.etymonline.com/index.php?term=god and http://www.etymonline.com/abbr.php, November, 2001.

16. http://www.eliyah.com/yhwhdss.html, *Yahweh's Name in the Dead Sea Scrolls*.

17. Gertoux, Gérard, The Name of God Y.eH.oW.aH Which is Pronounced As It Is Written I_EH_OU_AH, (Oxford: University Press of America, 2002), 4.

18. Nancy L. deClaisse-Walford, Biblical Hebrew, (St. Louis: Chalice Press, 2002), 1.

19. The HarperCollins Bible Dictionary, (San Francisco: Harper Collins Publishers, 1996), 736.

20. Thomas Brisco, *Holman Bible Atlas*, (Nashville: Broadman& Holman Publishers, 1998), 176.

21. ISBE, Vol 4, 157.

22. The Works of Josephus, William Whiston, A.M., translator, (Peabody, MA: Hendrickson Publishers, 1987), 71.

23. ISBE, Vol 4, 400.

24. Please note that in the King James translations, Exodus 6:3 has Elohim's name translated as Jehovah and not Yahwah. Even though the correct Hebrew pronunciation of Elohim's name, YHWH is not known, it is pretty certain that Jehovah is not correct. The Hebrew alphabets did not include any letters that had the "j" sound. On the other hand, the initial consonant in the name is a "y" which is the "y" sound.

25. Matthew Henry, Rev. Leslie F. Church, Ph.D. ed., "Commentary on the Whole Bible by Matthew Henry", (Grand Rapids: Zondervan Publishing House, 1961), 1642.

26. Exodus 23:14-17 "Three times a year you shall celebrate a feast to Me. You shall observe the Feast of Unleavened Bread; for seven days you are to eat unleavened bread, as I commanded you, at the appointed time in the month Abib, for in it you came out of Egypt. And none shall appear before Me empty-handed. Also *you shall observe* the Feast of the Harvest *of* the first fruits of your labors *from* what you sow in the field; also the Feast of the Ingathering at the end of the year when you gather in *the fruit of* your labors from the field. Three times a year all your males shall appear before the Lord GOD.

27. Baal means lord. This is the name of the principal god of the Phoenicians and is found several times in the Scriptures as the name for the mighty ones served by the people living around the Israelties. The plural is Baalim. Many times in the Scriptures the word Baal precedes the name of a place,

indicating that the mighty one served or worshiped in that particular location. See Numbers 25:3, Deuteronomy 4:3.

28. New Revised Standard Version Bible (New York: Oxford University Press, 1989), xv.

29. ISBE, Vol 3, 481.

30. G. H. Parke-Taylor, Yahweh: The Divine Name in the Bible (Waterloo, Ontario: Wilfrid Laurier University Press, 1975), 3.

31. See Leviticus 24:22; Leviticus 25:17, 38, 55; Leviticus 26:1, 2,13, 44, 45; Numbers 3:14, 41, 45; Numbers 10:10; Numbers 14:35; Numbers 15:41; Numbers 18:20; Numbers 35:34; Deuteronomy 5:6, 9; and Deuteronomy 29:6.

32. See also Acts 2:21 and Romans 10:31. Despite what some falsely teach, the name referenced is none other than the name of YHWH, the Heavenly Father. The Prophet Joel is being quoted by Peter in his speech found in Acts 2 and Paul is also quoting the same source in his letter to the Romans.

About The Author

Iris A. Foreman is an avid student and teacher of the Old Testament scriptures. She earned a B.S. in Political Science from Lincoln University and an M.B.A. from Drexel University. After a rewarding career in financial management in both the private and public sectors, she returned to school to further her biblical studies. It was then that she received a Master of Divinity degree from Regent University. For several years, she has been researching the Hebrew Scriptures, Christian doctrine, and church history.

In addition to studying, writing, and teaching, she is the executive director for the Foundation for Hospice, a nonprofit agency that provides assistance to terminally ill individuals who lack the necessary resources to die in dignity, peace, and comfort.

She currently lives in North Carolina with her husband Anthony, son Sydney, and her two dogs, Colby and Jordan.